Charlie
Simpson's
Apocalypse

Charlie Simpson's Apocalypse

Joe Eszterhas

RANDOM HOUSE
New York

Library of Congress Cataloging in Publication Data

Eszterhas, Joe.
  Charlie Simpson's apocalypse.

  1. United States—Social conditions—1960–
—Case studies. 2. Simpson, Charles R., 1947–1972.
3. Conflict of generations. 4. Murder—United States
—Case studies.
HN59.E84   309.1'73'092   73–5036
ISBN 0–394–48424–X

Manufactured in the United States of America
98765432
First Edition

For my father
and Geri

Charlie Simpson's Apocalypse

I
Mad-Dog
Dance

THEY *are plainsmen who live in the teeth of the wind, ever alert for its deathroar. They eyeball the skies and stock jerrybuilt cyclone cellars with candles, flashlight, and the Holy Bible. At dusk in mid-May, fifteen years ago, thirty-six of them died, two hundred were injured. The whirlwind came at 6:12, its funnel a dazzling-white smokestack. The sun was setting; there was little hail or lightning.*

It raked up a hedge fence near Williamsburg, stripped homes naked, uprooted trees. Dirt and debris stained the funnel. By the time it gutted Antioch Cemetery outside Homewood, it was a blood-trailing maneater. Rotation speed: 200 m.p.h. Length of main path: 71 miles. Length of secondary path: 7 miles. Width: four-tenths of a mile.

It bulldozed the ancient Civil War graveyard and tossed slabs like sandpebbles—a tombstone was found in a hayloft nine miles away. It roared like hell's own sonic boom; its funnel was a whopping skybound chameleon: black, yellow, green, orange, dirty gray. Outside Ottawa, it "sorta stood still, backed up, and do-se-doed like partners in a square dance." It rode the concrete of U.S. 50 and, in less than sixty seconds, did a million dollars' damage to a motel, four houses, a truckstop, seven tractor-trailers, and a Drive-In Theater. Trapped by fallen powerlines, a sheriff's deputy sat paralyzed in his cruiser and watched the earth burn around him. A 500-gallon watertank was blown from its truck a mile into an apple orchard.

Its funnel stuffed with turkeys, sheep, pigs, lumber, tires, and metal, it spinned off U.S. 50 and met a cattle-truck headon. The driver leaped from his cab into a ditch pooled with rain. His rig went to the right, his cab to the left. The ditch was sucked dry. Stretched flat, his face in the mud, the driver survived. "God had his hand on my shoulder," he said.

The purple sunball sank lower; the whirlwind pre-empted the sky. It demolished twenty-two homes in a 3-mile radius. It slashed the Springfield Cemetery to bits and swept two little girls from their dinner table, discarding them among dead pigs, twisted fenders, and desecrated graves.

At 7:53, it blew itself out over the wheatfields and faded into twilight. Sirens wept; volunteer firemen scavenged the land with bodybags and spotlights.

IT'S getting so that a man can't live in peace anywhere, not even on his own plot of land. Harrisonville, Missouri, is forty miles southeast of Kansas City along I-71, ten minutes down the blacktop from the redbrick farmhouse where Harry S Truman, President and haberdasher, was born. Life should be staid and bucolic, a somnolent leftover of what everyone who buys the $3.00 Wednesday night catfish dinner at Scott's Bar B-Q calls Them Good Old Days. But it isn't like that anymore. There's always some botheration to afflict a man these days . . . the velvetleaf that ravaged the soybeans last year . . . horse-thieves who drive the gravel roads in BigCity semis rustling lazyboned old nags . . . or them vagrant tornadoes.

They call the lush area Twister Alley. Of all the woebegone acreage in America, Harrisonville and the fastblink jerkwater towns clustered about it—Peculiar, Lone Jack, Gunn City—attract more funnel clouds each hardluck year than anyplace else. Folks have learned some things about meteorology: When horses gather in a fieldcorner, it's going to rain. When cows bellow at night, it's going to hail. When pigs carry straws to their sty, the funnel is near. The storms sweep across green-backed rows of wheat and corn, raising holy hell two or three times a year with the insurance rates and the little money a farming man has after Uncle Sam takes his bagman's share . . . Couple years ago, for example, the Lake Luna Dam threatened to crack and drown the crops. The whole town was out there with sandbags when the sirens went off; folks left the dam and fled to their cellars. The twister tore through, leaving two inches of rain. The dam burst; floodwater covered the trees and fences the tornado had toppled . . . For some Godforsaken reason, the terrain prickteases these choleric storms, and out around a campfire on a warm spring night, a man can sit with his Red Fox or Mail Pouch and wait for jagged strips of lightning to neon the wisteria and the hollyhock.

Except for the twisters, it is like any other tacky jaundiced Southern town. Once home of the Osage Indians, it carries a hidebound but atrophied Dixie tradition—though it is not far from the Kansas bordertown where John Brown, revolutionary utopian murderer, launched his bloodbath a century ago. Billy Quantrill's Yankee-hating raiders once bushwhacked here; Cole Younger's daddy was the town's second mayor. Cole himself rode with the Dalton Brothers, who were born on Holmes Road, and with Jesse James, patron-saint of the town's poorfolk . . . Jesse once robbed a bank in the middle of town and when his horse threw a shoe during the getaway, he dismounted without an eyebat and told the blacksmith to shoe her . . . Carry Nation grew up a few miles away, on High Blue Trail, and so did know-it-all Dale Carnegie, buried with flinty old Carry in the graveyard off Highway 58 between High Blue and Belton. Harry "Harricula" Truman, or just plain Harry S (as they say at Scott's Bar B-Q) visited one Appreciation Day not long after he dropped the Aye-Tomic Bomb. Harry chewed saucy chicken legs on the courthouse steps and said the White House was a big white jail.

There was never much criminal excitement, and the most celebrated gunfire in the town's history was its very first murder —in the summer of 1871—when Tom Sabena, scion of one of the best families, went berserk on the square, killing a constable and a farmer, spraying bullets, until a merchant cut him down with a double-barreled coyote gun. The other murders were nothing to speak of: a knife-fight over thirty head of cattle, a cuckolding wife bludgeoned by her sectionhand husband. There were a few burglaries and two jailbreaks: the first in 1936, when the Rev. Perry E. Griffin fled arm-in-arm with his jazzy harlot lover; the second in 1937, when a bankteller who'd embezzled $340 chopped a hole in the jail roof with a pocketknife. The embezzler's escape was embarrassing: it took place while the town was celebrating its 100th anniversary with a foxchase, a soap box derby, and a pet parade. Thanks to the man's trusty pocketknife, a new jail was built.

The biggest early twentieth-century excitement was caused by the motorcar, driven down from Kansas City by a doctor in 1901 and parked on the square, where it attracted the mayor and half the town. By 1906, residents were writing letters of alarm to the Cass County *News:* "I consider the auto a dangerous vehicle and I do not feel safe with my family. I know of many persons who do not trade in Harrisonville because of the autos being used" . . . "My folks are afraid to drive to Harrisonville on account of the motor cars" . . . "Why is it that our hitchtracks are not crowded as they once were? Automobiles are killing the town. There are more vacant houses than ever before."

The town's self-concept stayed constant. In 1937, the Chamber of Commerce made a centennial announcement: "The sterling integrity and able business qualifications of the leading men have developed the town with credit. We invite all peoples to a clean well-governed town. Good streets and granitoid sidewalks all over, electric lights, telephone, water-works system. Transportation here is unrivaled, with four main lines of railroad diverging in all directions. It is a delightful and pleasant place to make a home. For business, for home comforts, for investments,

Harrisonville stands without equal. The center of a great country, the home of a God-loving and God-serving people, her churches and schools speak loudly of the culture and character of her people." Thirty-four years later, on the 31st of December, 1971, a halfpage ad in the Cass County *Democrat-Missourian* said: "There's some folks who are always talking about 'Good Old Days.' Why not? They were good. The best of the past and present have made this community such a wonderful place to live. We've preserved parts of our cherished heritage. We've moved ahead into excitingly new concepts of business and industry. Our town? It's the greatest!" It was signed: "G.M. Allen, president-of-bank, firechief, school board member, Chamber of Commerce member."

Harrisonville (population 4,700) serves as Cass County's seat and by 1980 will be only a few miles south of the exact demographic center of America, a frogleap away from the very heart of the calcified Heartland. It is a footnote which greatly pleases the town's flaccid watery-eyed mayor and dentist, Dr. M.O. Raine. As the sun started warming in the spring of 1972 and the last snowfall was shoveled away on April Fool's Day, folks were getting ready for the summer: The Harrisonville Fire Department wail-tested its six Civil Defense Air Raid/Tornado Warning sirens and even the corniced Harrisonville Hotel, the oldest building in town, its roof scarred by generations of funnel clouds, got a homey facelift. Its eroded brick was scraped and washed down. The World's Largest Santa Claus, standing thirty feet tall, wearing six-foot boots, and overlooking fifty thousand pines in Christmas Tree Lane on Number Seven Highway, got his beard repainted. The Missouri Turkey-Shoot Season was opening; the American Legion Hall at 303 Pearl Street, a mausoleum of cigarbutts, housed a nightly claphappy gospel meeting—"Do You Want To Be Saved?"—and the Peculiar Panthers knocked off the favored Harrisonville Wildcat basketball team, 66-55, erasing a string of twenty-five straight regional Wildcat triumphs.

The Chamber of Commerce announced "real big, real good" news: the long-delayed acquisition of a shiny chrome-jeweled 1972 ambulance. Husky George Van Antwerp, a bespectacled volunteer fireman, got his picture in the *Democrat-Missourian*, giving an oxygen mask a mouth-splitting smile. Organized in 1923 by the American Legion, the fire department now had eight vehicles to combat any emergency: the ambulance, a rescue truck equipped with highbeam spotlight, a brush buggy to battle grassfires, a tanker, and four pumpers. It had thirty-two blaze-hungry volunteer firemen, all of them Legionnaires.

Less than a month after the twin-stretchered new ambulance got its first exalted whirls around the town square, on a muggy thunderheaded warm day, Friday, April 21st, at 5:55 P.M., the Civil Defense sirens let out a high-pitched shriek that cut across the fields for miles around. Folks hurried to their citizens' band radios to await emergency instructions.

They thought it was another goddamn ruckus-raising tornado.

They couldn't understand the breathless disjointed words which G.M. Allen—bank president, school board member, Chamber of Commerce member, firechief—garbled at his white-helmeted Legionnaire volunteers in the hamlets and hollows around town.

What in tarnation was G.M. talking about?

"Hippies . . . Killed two policemen . . . Dead . . . M-1 carbine . . . Blood all over town . . . the Simpson boy . . . Come on into town . . . There's more of 'em . . . Yo, a revolution!"

ON Friday, April 21st:

Astronaut John W. Young leaped off the moondust and exuberantly saluted the American flag. At North Carolina State University, a thousand college kids snakedanced around a hand-painted sign that said: "Nixon's Machine is Falling." In Lawrence, Kansas, the scene of past bloody street-actions, six hundred persons met in front of Strong Hall, the University of Kansas Administration Building, to plan an anti-war march the next day.

At 5:50 P.M., on the town square in Harrisonville, Charlie Simpson, twenty-five years old, 6 foot 3, 180 pounds, flowing shoulder-length gunmetal-black hair, known to his friends as "Ootney," leaped out of a red Volkswagen. He was an asthmatic who admired Henry David Thoreau and had coalblack diamond-hard eyes shaped like razor-slits. The car was driven by a friend, John Risner, twenty-six, a pallid Navy veteran, the son of a former deputy sheriff, beer-bellied, wire-bearded, blue-jeaned. Risner wore a picaresque blackfelt English derby hat. The car had a peace symbol on its windshield.

Charlie Simpson jumped out of the car on Independence Street, less than a thousand feet from the Allen Bank and Trust Company, a modernized plateglass structure facing the court-house. Simpson, a farmboy who lived in the apple-knocker village of Holden twenty-four miles away, started walking south on Independence. He wore knee-popped bellbottom jeans, a waist-length

Army fatigue jacket, and yellowed dry-goods boots caked with mud and cowflop. He had high jutting cheekbones, a hooked and fist-kissed nose, a swarthy complexion, and uneven calcimine-white teeth. He suddenly crossed the street and started running. There was whipcord in his muscles but he looked awkward when he ran. It was more a self-conscious and deerlike lope.

As he loped across Independence onto Pearl Street, Charlie Simpson reached under his patched Army jacket and bared an M-1 semi-automatic with clip. He'd used the combat-regulation weapon in the fields around town with his friend Rise Risner, target-shooting overfed squirrels, moonlighting packrats, and non-returnable bottles of Budweiser beer. Using an M-1 on a packrat, he'd said to Rise, was like blowing it apart with a grenade. It was the same-type weapon which Ohio National Guardsmen used at Kent State in 1970, when they killed four students and wounded nine others.

On this Friday afternoon, as Charlie Simpson reached for the M-1 under his Army jacket, he saw two brown-uniformed members of the Harrisonville Police Department—Donald Marler, twenty-six, and Francis Wirt, twenty-four—walking toward him. They were part of the department's Foot Patrol, recently pressured by town businessmen to keep a whiphand on the square. Both men were armed with holstered police regulation .38s. Both men knew Simpson. Wirt was a Vietnam veteran, back from the war only four months and a policeman less than one.

As Friday-afternoon traffic backed up around the quarter-pointed square—stores were closing and each of the square's four corners is stoplighted—Charlie Simpson leaned into a crouch and leveled his semi-automatic carbine waist-high at the two policemen. They were less than a hundred feet away. He squeezed a brief burst of bullets. People in their cars a few feet from him— the streets around the square are so narrow they form a continuous alleylike one-way—heard the gunfire, saw the two policemen go down poleaxed, and threw themselves flatchested to the cobblestoned pavement. A florid macawlike spinster twenty feet from the gunfire fainted and her car rammed the Happiness-Is-Tastee-Freeze delivery truck in front of her.

Simpson ran toward the two policemen sprawled on the concrete. Both were moaning, bleeding badly, their holsters still buckled, unable to return fire. He stood as stiff as a scarecrow over both men, pointing the muzzle down over first one and then the other—"Don't shoot me!" Marler screamed, "God! Oh God!"—and fired two staccato bursts into their bodies at point-blank range. The bullets made for warzones ripped into and through the bodies. Marler was hit twice in the chest, twice in the abdomen, and once in each hand. Wirt was hit twice in the abdomen and three times in the right arm. His elbow looked like it had been fragged.

Simpson spinned, turned to the Allen Bank and Trust Company, and dashed inside. He was a death-dealing whirligig. He said nothing. He had a shitfire grin on his face. He didn't aim the carbine at anyone. He pointed it willy-nilly toward a rear wall covered with money-saving slogans—"Invest in America, Buy U.S. Savings Bonds"—and fired again. Bullets ricocheted around the floor and walls, wounding two bookkeepers. Mary Ellen Stuart, twenty-two, said: "I didn't recognize the sound. I thought it was a car backfiring or something. Then I looked up into the lobby and saw him standing in front, firing. I pushed Mrs. Roach down behind my desk. When the shooting stopped, Mrs. Roach said: 'I think I've been shot.' She had blood on the back of her dress. After the man left I stood up and saw that I had blood on my side and realized I'd been shot, too."

Simpson turned again, ran outside, waving the rifle in front of him like a cheerleader's baton, and zigzagged west on Pearl, heading toward the town's water tower—"Hi there! Class of '69" —and the Cass County sheriff's office, where crewcut and fleshy Sheriff Bill Gough, forty-six years old, was just going off duty. The sheriff's office is a thousand feet west on Pearl Street from the Allen Bank. Across the street from Gough's office is the Capitol Cleaners, which monopolizes the town's laundry trade, offers "Starch Bargains," and is decorated with a heavy flapping sign that promises "More Top Value Stamps."

As Charlie Simpson dashed from the bank to the sheriff's office down the narrow street, a 58-year-old man with boils on his neck named Orville T. Allen was stepping out of his battered 1968 white Ford station wagon in front of the cleaners. He'd managed a dry-cleaning store in Garden City for twenty-seven years and was there to pick up some part-time weekend laundry.

Charlie Simpson saw Orville Allen across the street, a dour-faced man in faded khaki pants he'd never seen before, and aimed his carbine. The burst tattooed Allen across the chest. He dropped to the pavement, twisted in the gutter, turned his bleeding chest to the sky, and clasped his hands in prayer. "Lord," he moaned. Blood trickled across the street toward the sheriff's office.

Sheriff Gough, hulking and slow-footed, had just taken off his holstered .38 revolver and was reading that week's issue of the *Democrat-Missourian*. The paper had come out at noon and carried a front-page story about a Kansas teenager the sheriff's deputies had arrested for possession of marijuana. Gough heard something *rat-tat-tat!* outside his office as he scanned the paper, but didn't think it was gunfire. He thought it sounded like some fool drumming on a piece of tin. He hurried outside, annoyed and cussing, to see what the hell the commotion was about.

He saw Simpson dancing toward him, the M-1 aimed head-high. He tried to duck but wasn't quite fast enough (although the savage reflexlike twist of his big body probably saved his life). He was hit in the right shoulder and left leg but staggered inside his office. His wife, sitting at a desk, screamed. He knocked her to the floor, grabbed his revolver, and flung himself behind a desk with such force that his elbows were purple for weeks. Covered with his own blood, the sheriff aimed the revolver at the door and waited for Simpson to open it. His hands trembled. He was afraid he'd lose control, afraid his fingers would twitch the trigger before Simpson stuck his head inside.

When he hit Gough in the street, Simpson wheeled, and waving the carbine wildly, trotted back toward the square. Then, in front of the Harrisonville Retirement Home, a dim matchboxed grayslab building across the street from Orville Allen's bleeding body, Charlie Simpson stopped. He bent down, put the carbine into his mouth, and sucked the barrel like a popsickle. He fired his last burst. He blew the top of his head off. His mad-dog dance was over; treacly tissue flecked the Retirement Home walls.

He'd fired more than forty rounds. Four people were dead, three wounded. The town's snazzy new Chamber of Commerce ambulance paraded around the square collecting bodies and gobbets of flesh. The oxygen mask George Van Antwerp had showcased on the front page dripped with gooey catarrhal fluid and blood. As the Civil Defense sirens screamed and G.M. Allen's volunteer firemen hosed away the bloodpools, gunwielding deputies and policemen grabbed all the longhairs around the square and marched them to Bill Gough's jail.

"**ALL** roads lead to the square," an editorial in J.W. Brown's shopping-news weekly, the Cass County *Democrat-Missourian*, once said. "At least that's what it seems like to outsiders. The square seems to us to be a big chunk out of the past sitting in the middle of the present. The cobblestoned streets, the old hotel and courthouse, are probably taken for granted by the townspeople."

Charlie Simpson's fierce assault on the Harrisonville square was the final escalation of a guerilla war of raw nerves and icy glares. It was fought for control of a seemingly insignificant logistical area: courthouse steps, shrubbery encircling it, and sidewalks facing its entrances on Wall and Pearl streets. To understand the fated intensity of this cornponed guerilla war, one must understand the uniquely claustrophobic architecture of the square itself as well as its place in Harrisonville's rustic/schizoid tradition.

The courthouse anchors the square, surrounded on four sides by contrasting clapboard and imitation brick shops. It is the center of a tight and walled-in quadrangle decorated by flags, butterflies, and parking meters. The cobblestone pavement on the four streets surrounding it—Wall to the south, Lexington to the east, Pearl to the north, Independence to the west—is chokingly narrow. It is less than thirty feet from the courthouse curb to the businesses on its sides. The streets were designed for horse and buggies, not delivery trucks. All the streets are one-way in a looping arc; you have to drive through Lexington and Pearl to get to Independence. Since the streets are so tight, the shops on all sides—like South Side Prescriptions, Felix Hacker's Paint Supplies, Ballon's Dry Goods, Wright's Shoe Palace—are but an armstretch away from whatever is happening around the courthouse. If someone sitting on the courthouse steps shouts "Off The Pigs!" for example, the words will be dramatically echo-chambered, reverberating through the little stores where, in years past, only the cash registers made noise.

The courthouse was erected in 1897 at a cost of $45,000 (paid in two years by direct taxation), replacing the old one, built in 1835 and used as a stable by the invading Union Army. It is of carefully tended redbrick, three stories high, topped by a cupolaed belltower and a flapole. The bells ring once a year—on the Fourth of July. The flagpole is bare; a new one splits the grass in front of the WarVets statue and flies the flag twenty-four hours a day. The building stands atop a moundlike elevation exactly sixteen steps above the neatly swept sidewalks. A black iron railing leads to the south side doors, which are flanked by four graystone columnar pillars. The elevation transforms the courthouse into a stage. If Old Lloyd Foster, for example, who ebulliently runs South Side Prescriptions, glances out his storewindow at the courthouse, he is looking *up*. The building is at the tip of his nose: Old Lloyd's got a front-row pantoscopic view.

On the Wall Street side of the courthouse is a fixed metal sign that says: "Learn to Lead! Army NCO Candidate School." The same kind of sign on the Independence Street side in red-white-blue says: "The Marine Corps Builds Men! 2735 B Troop." Six feet of manicured grass and shrubbery surround the building on all sides. The clock atop the belltower is dead. It's been stuck for more than a decade. ("We can't afford to get it fixed," a councilman says.) The clock's hands paralyzed at different times

—it is 2.20 to the south, 6:25 to the east, 1:20 to the west. The northern clockface has been removed; pigeons flutter there. A deeply carved inscription above the southern door says: "A Public Office Is A Public Trust."

The courthouse steps and the town square have served for generations as a place of public lolling, a spot to rest, dangle your bunions, and soak the sun. In Them Good Old Days, Saturday night hoedowns were celebrated there; its four streets were saw-horsed and dressed up with multicolored lightbulbs. Three times a year there was a carnival complete with cotton candy, candied apples, and a horseshoe-pitching contest. And gradually the town fathers—meaning the bankers, aldermen, and Chamber of Commerce officials—accepted too that the courthouse steps and shrubbery served as a haven for grizzled Retirement Home winos to gulp their pints of Missouri cornwhiskey. Every smalltown has its drunks; they are harmless loathsome examples to contrast with Godfearing lives. The old bullshit artists tilt sweatstained hats over their mooneyes, keep their bottles near their bellies, and are happy enough to be left alone. They exude alcohol and sour courtesy, fuss no one, and judges shake their heads and walk smugly past them to mahoganied chambers where crystal decanters of Jack Daniel's are kept out of sight.

In the fall of 1971 the town drunks abandoned the court-house steps and claimed they were being spooked out. The figures now lazing in the shade and dangling their legs were a bewildering new phenomenon. They were kids. They were townie kids who'd grown up around Cass County and played for the Harrisonville Wildcats, getting their first treasured packs of prophylactics from tight-lipped Lloyd Foster. But when Old Lloyd looked across at these homegrown kids now, they stood his hair on end. They were different. They'd changed. They were their own kids but, criminy! they weren't their own kids anymore, either. They wore their hair Adam's apple long and frazzled and grew mongol mustaches down to their chins, and Fidel Castro beards. Some of them looked about as homely as a stump fence built in the dark. They were ragged out in all manners of beegum strawhats and cropduster outfits—always the same slattery bluejeans and a lot of Army jackets, engineers' boots, and $2 tenny-shoes which Old Lloyd's son, Don, sold them at the Sears Country Catalog store. They were unwashed and uncombed and acted brazen-faced and biggity. They played knockabout Frisbee in the middle of the street, garbage-collected wilted flowers in back of Vann's Florist Shop, and decked themselves out with dead roses and carnations. They wore "love crosses" around their necks from which Jesus's body had been blasphemously torn away. They unzipped their constantly halfstaff flies and pissed on the WarVets statue and the time-honored bailey wall.

Some of the women who came once a week to Connie's Beauty Salon said they gave them googoo eyes, called them vile names, and scratched their privates, laughing like sexcrazy perverts. Some of the policemen said they called them "pigs" face-to-face and carried on about their godalmighty Civil Liberties. Some of the businessmen claimed the single word they heard uglifying the square from morning till they turned on the burglar alarm was a four-letter word they couldn't even repeat with women and children around. Their historic square was degenerating into a place of profanity, heathenism, and concupiscence; the sober business of law was being conducted right atop Harrisonville's own newsprung Tenderloin. "There was no doubt about it," says sixty-year-old J.W. Brown, dealer in certitudes, editor and publisher of the *Democrat-Missourian*, a flatulent pipe-puffing country gentleman. "What we had were our own hippies, setting up there, raising hell, calling our women names, drinking wine and smoking some of that marijuana. I even heard tell they was right up there in the bushes having sexual intercourse. Yes sir, Sex-You-All intercourse. Now those old drunks who used to set up there, those old boys never did any of that."

Sex-You-All debauchery sixteen steps above ground level at the nosetips of sanctimonious town merchants is not exactly what the new courthouse squatters had in mind. They were there in the beginning partly because there was no other place to go. Where could you go in Harrisonville?—this smalltime place haunted by homilies, platitudes, and booshwah. Into Guido's Pizza Parlor? Well, maybe, but you couldn't stay there too long. As time went by, Win Allen, the kingpin, Rise Risner, Ootney Simpson, George Russell, Harry Miller, and the Thompson Brothers hung around the square because it got to be a showboating mock-serious game. They were liberating Harrisonville, showing the hypocrites and phonies and $$$-squirrelers and chokeragged Yesmen some puffed-up balls. They were widening the mental horizons of a town more narrow-minded than its streets; they were missionaries laboring among their bloodkin: moneytheistic theocentric cousins and uncles who swore allegiance to Uncle Sam, Jim Crow, Oral Roberts, and Dale Carnegie; they were waging their impudent revolution against people they'd cowedly called "sir" all their teenage lives.

Beer-bellied Rise Risner and Gary Hale, reedy and subdued, his eyes like leadshot, went off to the Navy cowlicked country boys —"I enlisted in a moment of temporary insanity," Rise says—and came back dazedly turned-on, rejecting everything around them. They were home . . . but home sure as hell didn't feel like home.

"I was born here and I lived here all my life," says Rise, "until I went into the military. I was in from April of '67 to January of '71. All the rest of the time I've lived here. When we were growing up, we didn't really know anything. I was totally ignorant of everything till like, '69. That's the first time I ever did any chemicals. I was frosted, man! I thought all my life there was just one thing to do: Get a job. Get married. All that cheapshit. I just changed overnight and I kept learning from there, learning all kinds of shit."

"I moved here when I was in the fifth grade," Gary Hale mutters, "and I wasn't aware of my surroundings till I was in the service and found out what life was really like. I was off the coast of Nam and I was on a ship. I hated the service and I hated getting back."

Rise laughs: "We immediately started drawing unemployment when we got back here. First thing, you know, really having fun. I knew what was going down. I felt like a dwarf with seven humps, man, when I got back but I kind of mingled in. I know now that I knew The Truth! but I wasn't into it all that deep, yet I did know The Truth! and I saw through a lot of shit. Like I could see through the phony bullshit in a lot of people and I could see what they really were. I'd read a couple books by Abbie Hoffman and I read some Communist books and I knew there was definitely something going on that I wanted to be into. The book that made the biggest difference was Abbie Hoffman's. I took him very seriously and he wrote it in a way that I knew he'd been there before. He wasn't talking out of his ass. He'd gone through those riots and shit and really seen it. I just trusted the man to be telling the truth. We hated everything back then, we hated the way everything was run, but we're just now learning to do something about it."

Liberating Harrisonville meant a lot of hoky vaudevillian mind-blowing. They found themselves idolized romantic figures, scapegrace-superstars, fawned over by some of the high school kids, especially girls, the same way they themselves asskissed their own idiot/saints: Abbie Hoffman and Jerry Rubin. They conducted hoohawing teach-ins in front of the WarVets statue for clusters of mind-hungry teenagers (as Legionnaires stood around the sidewalk saying it was "jackrolling the blind" and the whole world was "going to hell in a handbasket"). They read selections from Abbie and Jerry, Tim Leary, Bobby Seale, in stentorian tones, lifting their decibel-level in phrases like "Off the pigs!" and "Up against the wall, motherfucker!" They kept Dylan and Jimi Hendrix tapes in their cars and boomed "Stone Free" and "Lay Lady Lay" into the night. They smoked as much dope as was available and there was always more than enough: the Army planted crops of hemp during WWII and five-foot-high marijuana plants played peekaboo with the wheatfields. Snake-charmed, the high school kids started imitating them, using words like "motherfucker" and acting heavylidded stoned in civics class for the sheer pleasure and aggravation of it. The principal, an ex-Marine, freaked, heroically and publicly, and zeroed in on new villains at council meetings where the school budget was discussed and the vandalism dollar-damage was totaled. He canceled the contract of a matronly English teacher who made Heinlein's *Stranger in a Strange Land* required reading. The townspeople soon grokked the taboo: the lady was once seen going into a liquor store and the town Wise Ones gossiped she was an out-and-out draggle-tail, fucksucking the seniors in her classes.

So these ragtag plowboy hippies—who were convinced their elders still cornholed cows when they permitted themselves to get horny—came to dominate the town's consciousness and its lethargic legendary square, scandalizing folks who still had to buy their booze in liquor stores because the bars only sell beer. Of all the revolutionaries and sugartits cavorting around the square, two seemed the most frightening: the Simpson boy, who'd rub his secret parts like a hog in heat when a lady walked near, and The Nigger, so low that a cockroach couldn't crawl under him. Diminutive Win Allen, twenty-four, frail and birdlike, with constantly bloodshot hooded eyes and a habit of slurring his words, was a dashiki-wearing Bad Nigger, as opposed to his younger brother, Butch, a walking bowling ball, who played forward for the Harrisonville Wildcats, scored an average 15 points per game, and was a Good Nigger. But this loutish Win (short for Edwin), had an Afro-bush popout hairdo and said the most violent Un-American things in a quiet lisping miss-nancyish way. Worse, he was always up there on the steps, holding hands and mushing with some bedeviled white high school girl, talking about Love, and waving frayed books like "Revolution For The Hell Of It!" and "Do It!" Every time one of Bill Davis's policemen or Bill Gough's deputies passed the square, Win Allen would cheerfully yell: "Hey, here comes The Pigs!"

He even spoke his own private blackevil language, and soon half the kids in high school were using this garbled childrenese, not just ordinary hippie words the townspeople heard on TV commercials, but aberrant words they'd never heard before. Bilgewater words like "bro" for brother, "gritting down" for eating, "crib" for home, "P-ing down" for sexual intercourse, "skunk" for girl, and "bogosity" for anything he disagreed with. But the single phrase which all the kids were using was plain macaronic gibberish. When Win Allen liked anything as much as he liked P-ing down, he said: "Most ricky-tick." "Most ricky-tick" was heard all over town; a high school senior even used it in an essay on "The Prospect of Marriage."

The townspeople went home at night, after enduring the raucous courthouse shenanigans all day, and their own kids sassed them with "bogosity" and "gritting down" and "most ricky-tick." Firm action clearly had to be taken and the Chamber of Commerce stenciled and distributed a series of "suggestions": "Insist that the City Council adopt new model ordinances that will hold up in court. The last time the city ordinances were updated was in the 1930's. Changes in society and court rulings have made many of the ordinances unenforceable . . . Support our local law enforcement officials. Give them your personal assurance that you are behind them all the way. Help to generate a better community image and spirit of cooperation with them . . . Ask city council to hire additional police to specifically watch problem groups. The mere physical presence of police at their favorite spots will deter them, but this costs money, so be prepared to pay . . . Learn from the city police or county sheriff what is involved in making an arrest and gaining a conviction. Either city or county officials have jurisdiction . . . Identify and prosecute those who violate an ordinance. This takes guts and involvement but it is essential, for the police can't do it by themselves . . . Organize a local tip, turn-in-a-pusher program. Similar groups are proving quite effective in other cities . . . Make the square a less attractive gathering place. Groups primarily go there to gain public attention. Ignoring their antics will help. Trimming the shrubs and increasing the nightlights will make a major difference too . . . Let the merchants around the square know of your lack of safety while shopping there. A concerned citizenry is an effective deterrent and so far there is no unity among the merchants, but when it begins to affect their business more than it already has, they will begin to take action."

A special Chamber of Commerce meeting was held and G.M. Allen, cocalorum firechief, the town's chief cook and bottle washer, got up and spoke with hawkshaw eloquence: "I'm an American, damn it! And I'm proud to be an American! And I don't go for all this hanging the flag upside-down stuff!" But G.M. Allen had another reason for urging unilateral civic action, a pocketbook reason that threatened the prosperity and very salutariness of Harrisonville. The town was facing its biggest dollar threat since 1949, when the Mid-Continent Foundry went into bankruptcy and ninety people lost their jobs. Win Allen and Charlie Simpson and Rise Risner and their pestiferous claque had become an economic menace. Business was off all over the place, from the Capot Department Store to Alderman Luke Scavuzzo's grocery. (In 1968, John J. Ruddy, vice-president of Kansas City's J.C. Nichols Company, told the Chamber of Commerce: "You have to do something about your courthouse square. By the time future shopping centers with similar services and easier access are developed, it will be too late. Wider streets and public parking lots would maintain the trade.")

Why was business off? Simple enough, G.M. Allen said. The hippies! Some of the people who shuffled in to make their monthly mortgage payments to G.M. Allen's bank told him they were afraid to come into town. Because of the hippies! The hippies were terrorizing business away! The town just couldn't afford to sit around white-livered on its duff, shilly-shally, and let itself get overrun.

The aldermen concurred that action had become a matter of local survival, although one of them, sucking his teeth, pointed out alternatives—"Don't stretch the blanket now, G.M."—explaining the financial setback. There was a crippling nationwide economic crisis and wage-price freeze, and eleven miles down I-71 one of those deluxe glass and chromium shopping centers, calling itself Truman Corners, was booming. Maybe folks were shopping there because it boasted thousands of acres of parking space.

"Maybe so," G.M. snapped at the tooth-sucker, "but they'd be leaving their money here if it weren't for them hippies," and the City Council–Chamber of Commerce spring offensive to recapture the town square . . . for exiled old winos . . . was underway.

ACTUALLY, the town fathers mounted two simultaneous offensives on separate fronts, both under G.M. Allen's roosterlike command: Operations Hippie and Tornado. To facilitate the war against tornadoes, G.M. Allen thought it'd be a civic coup if the Firefighters Association of Missouri—tornado-watchers of the entire state!—held their annual convention in Harrisonville. The aldermen, perhaps contemplating the weekend revenue from five hundred firefighters and their middle-aged ladies, gratefully applauded G.M.'s boosterism. G.M. set the convention for Friday, April 21st. There would be a Tornado Committee meeting Saturday morning and a brassband parade Saturday afternoon. The merchants quickly cooperated and Doris's House of Charm announced it would offer a "Fireladies' Shampoo Special" for its beehive-headed lady tourists.

As a further step in Operation Tornado, G.M. ran off hundreds of emergency doomsday leaflets and distributed them in the stores around the square. His directive began: "When a torando is spotted in the Harrisonville area, six sirens around the city will sound a long blast for three minutes. Our air-raid emergency bombing warning differs from a storm warning by sounding an up-and-down warbling blast rather than a long continuing blast." It ended: "Take these precautions when a tornado approaches— 1. Take shelter in a storm cellar or underground excavation; 2. When underground shelter is not available, take shelter along the

/ 25

inside walls of a strongly reinforced building or under heavy furniture along an inside wall; 3. In open country, move away at right angles to the path of the approaching tornado. If there is no time to escape, lie flat in the nearest ditch or depression in order to avoid flying debris." It was signed: "BE ALERT! G.M. ALLEN, FIRECHIEF."

To facilitate Operation Hippie, G.M. argued it was necessary that everyone in town understand the critical vitiating nature of the crisis. He waged Psy-War, awwshucks style. He arranged with the Kiwanis Club to import a "drug addict expert." The "drug addict expert" was Robert Williams, police chief of the town of Grandview, a man of profound secondhand insight. Chief Williams heard about drugs and hippies all the time from his cop-pals in Kansas City. That made him an expert. "It's approaching a crisis stage," he turgidly told the Kiwanians. "Police can't even eliminate the problem. We've got to wake up and take a hard stand. What we've got to do is stand up and inject some old-fashioned moral values before all our young fall victim to those older marauders who prey on them." At the same time, the Harrisonville Community Betterment Council, doused by Chief Williams's scalding brainwater, appointed a Drug Abuse Committee. Its chairman: G.M. Allen.

Sheriff Bill Gough wrote a gospel-grinding flagwaving series in the *Democrat-Missourian*. The first part was headlined: "Parents, Know the Drug Threat! The Child You Save May Be Your Own!" "Marijuana," the sheriff wrote, "has long been in use in what we now term minority groups, but now it has spread across the land like cancer. Simple possession of marijuana is a felony that can be punished by jail terms of two to ten years or more. Drug use is without doubt becoming a way of life for some young people. And so, think about these things my friends! As adults, it is UP TO US TO HEAD THIS THING OFF IN OUR

COMMUNITY!" The sheriff appeared on the front page scowling at two garbage-bags filled with grass. The cutline said: "The arrests followed a call from an alert citizen who reported two men picking marijuana in a western Cass County field. The previous day sheriff's officers discovered another batch of marijuana being dried in an abandoned shed but were unable to discover who was drying it there. The sheriff advises farmers to keep a check on any abandoned buildings on their property."

Late at night, on the 23rd of March, G.M. Allen, a delegation of town businessmen, and members of City Council, met with police officials in G.M.'s bank, The Citizens' National on Wall Street. There was an ambience of cigar smoke and stale air. A list of crimes the hippies were suspected of was compiled; horror-stories culled from the participant/victims. . . . Someone broke into the courthouse one night by jimmying open a window. Nothing was stolen, but the criminal crept up three flights of stairs to the belltower. Nothing was damaged, but three felonious marijuana cigarette butts were found on the floor. . . . Several merchants claimed to have received anonymous phone calls. The caller used the word "motherfucker" and threatened "torching." . . . In nearby Archie, a carload of hippies were seen driving through and that same day bombthreats were reported at the Archie State Bank and the Archie Elementary School. . . . A twenty-two year-old housewife was raped by a blond longhaired hippie who asked to borrow a telephone book. The woman opened the door; the degenerate grabbed her and forced her into the kitchen. He threatened her with a waterglass and said he'd slit her open with a butcher-knife if she made any trouble. He fiendishly told her to put her infant to bed and then assaulted her on her bridal-shower sheets. The rapist was unshaven, wore tie-dyed bluejeans, black cowboy boots, and a wide dark-brown belt. The woman looked at the hippies on the square and said she couldn't identify any of them . . . which didn't mean one of their dope-smoking buddies in Kansas City didn't do it.

And they all knew, G.M. Allen said, about the obstruction of traffic on the square. Police Chief Davis knew, indeed he did. A young woman even made out a formal complaint, the chief told the meeting. One of the hippies had plopped across her carhood and wouldn't remove himself. Was Davis able to verify that? someone asked. "Well, not exactly," Davis said, "but we know it happened." Traffic was stopped umpteen times because of Frisbees sailing into the street. "But they walk out into the street right away and pick 'em up," a lawyer said. "Yeah, but that don't matter," Davis answered. "They're obstructing traffic, I don't care for how long."

Davis, a beefy man with a chipmunk's features and a sandpapery phlegm-coated voice, grew livid when he explained "what jacks me off the most." "They want to protest that war, hell, they wouldn't be able to set up there today if their daddies hadn't gone to war twenty-five years ago. Most of our kids wouldn't be getting into trouble if it weren't for them older guys who egg 'em on and put ideas inside their heads. They call themselves revolutionaries and that's what they are. They sure as hell aren't Americans." The ham in his jowls quivered like jello.

The mobilization meeting agreed on some immediate measures: shrubbery around the courthouse would be trimmed so there couldn't be any more dryhumping and fornicating up there. Superwatted bright lights, the kind used in urban highcrime areas, would be erected on all sides of the square. Chief Davis promised a new Foot Patrol: two of his nine officers would become robotized beatmen, walking up and down the tetragon twelve hours a day. A list of city ordinances—"Ordnances, man," Win Allen would say, "dig?"—was drawn up for City Council approval, the contribution of the toadying city attorney, a middle-aged man with punched-out eyes and belly.

"Vulgar, profane, or indecent" language in public was punishable by a $500 fine or sixty days in the county jail or both. "Imbibing intoxicating liquor in public" was punishable by the same penalty. Picketing and parades were illegal unless authorized by the city attorney or Police Chief Davis. And, a declaration of virtual martial law: Any gathering of three or more persons in the town square was an illegal assembly punishable by a $1,000 fine.

G.M. Allen, the little man with comic-book glasses and the Alfred E. Newman haircut that stopped a full inch above his redveined ears, was happy as a quahog. He had a responsibility as firechief/bank president/Chamber of Commerce member/red-blooded American, and he intended to live up to it. "You listen to TV, it used to be cowboys and Indians, now it's 'Kill the cops,' " he'd say. He was a World War II combat veteran who'd raised four decent lawabiding kids, and even though his youngest daughter had gone to school with Risner and Win Allen and liked them, even though she was "a little bit oversold on Civil Rights," G.M. Allen was convinced what they'd decided in his bank that night was for the betterment not only of Harrisonville, but of the United States of America. "Yes sir," he told the meeting, "if they don't believe in America, they ought to get the hell out!"

The next morning he was madder than a striped adder and twice as determined the town square was going to be reclaimed. Hours after the anti-Hippie/Frisbee/Promiscuity meeting, a thirty-pound slab of concrete crashed through the $495 plateglass window fronting G.M. Allen's bank. He sputtered half a block to see J.W. Brown at the *Democrat-Missourian* and ordered a bold-set black-bordered ad. He was petrified with emotion. The Citizens' National Bank was offering a $500 reward for "information leading to the arrest and conviction of the person or persons who maliciously broke our window."

For Win Allen, Rise Risner, Gary Hale, and Ootney Simpson, the "shit coming down from the black sky" was a routine part

of Life in the Hick City. They were pariahs beset by daily remind-
ers of their status. "Gary and I were hitch-hiking one time," Rise
says, "and we were sitting around in this coffee shop around ten
o'clock in the morning. We were just sitting in there when a
bunch of cowboys come in and ah, they didn't like us. This one
guy says to the waitress—'Hey, bring me a good sharp knife,
would you? I wanna cut some hair!' Another time we picked up
these two dudes outside town. They were hitch-hiking from New
Jersey. They said—'I don't care what you do, man, just get us out
of this state!' "

"I experienced a thing," Gary Hale says, lazing around the
words, "I was coming back from Ozark National Forest on a
Sunday evening. We'd been down there since Thursday and we
were coming back, three o'clock in the morning, a Monday morning. We passed through Carthage, Missouri, and the city police
pulled us over and they got us for—well, they stopped us for going
41 in a 40 m.p.h. zone. You know the reason they stopped us was
just some mean ballyraggin—it was the long hair and the beatup
car. At any rate they stopped us and shook us down and shook
the car down and they found a machete and a hatchet in the
backseat. They got us for concealed weapons. We were up in the
Ozarks, we needed the stuff to campout and chop shit down for
the fire, but they just busted us. We almost couldn't make bail."

"Looks like they can get away with anything," Rise says, his
voice bitter-edged. "Fuck, how can they get away with an ordinance saying you can't congregate more than three people in
town. And there's zero lawyers in town willing to help us. They're
all tied in together, they're all country jakes. The pigs give out a
ticket and the dude hires a lawyer in town. Fuck, the lawyers don't
care how many tickets the pigs give, it's all money in the Allen
Bank for all of 'em. Like there's not one person—not one fucking
influential person in town that can help us that will because they
all hate us.

"My old man used to be a deputy sheriff in this town," Rise says, "he's been there. He knows all the shit that goes on. It's common fact in this town that if you've got enough money you can buy your way out of anything, you don't even have to go to court. It's common knowledge who you see to pay off and this guy is a city official. A friend of mine got a Driving While Intoxicated. He went to see a lawyer and my friend gave the lawyer five hundred dollars and the lawyer made one phonecall and the DWI was knocked down to careless and imprudent driving and he didn't lose his license.

"It's common knowledge that people who got money can beat anything. Hell, they won't even ticket them in town. Everybody hates it, even the fucking rednecks hate it, but they go along with it cause they're scared. The pigs go to the city attorney and they say—'Well, we got a bunch of longhaired Communists up on the fucking streets and we want 'em off.' So the guy just sits back in his leatherchair and makes up an ordinance. I mean, fuck, Khrushchev was a saint compared to us. The pigs in this town are hired by the rich man to guard what the fuck the man's got—his house, his bank, all that cheapshit. We're basically country people, man. We're hillbillies. We're dumb. But we know when we're getting fucked-over and we don't like it. They call us Communists, bastards, degenerates, perverts, purvoids, and then we can't call 'em pigs 'cause we'll go to jail."

George Russell, twenty-four, short and curlyheaded, with long uneven sideburns and a bristly toothpick mustache, is reminded of his father. "It's like my father is a typical redneck, he's just a typical bummer farmer, and he says—'Well, I'm not prejudiced or anything.' Yet when I tell him, I say—'We're just today's niggers,' man, you talk about somebody getting pissed off, nothing like it. But he's not prejudiced against niggers at all . . . but me calling myself one, well that's different.

"You know, like I heard Lloyd Foster," says George Russell,

"the old guy who runs the drugstore. He told Win once—'Why don't you go back to your own country?' Hell, fucking Win was born in this country."

"Yeah," Win Allen laughs. It is a searing laugh that comes from the stomach. "Let me rub something on you. It's like this. Like an Irishman, he comes here, he stays an Irishman. An Eye-Talian, he comes here, he stays an Eye-Talian. But an African leaves Africa, ooohoo! they call us Noogrows! and Nigras! and Niggers! and then some old fart says to me—'Go back to your own country!' Now if that old fart Foster wants to play wordgames, he should call himself a Long Knife!"

During the second week of April, as the footpatrols made ten-minute-reconnaissance sorties around their turf and the outlaws were forced to scatter around the square in isolated pairs, Win Allen came up with what he told Charlie Simpson was "Dee-Vine Inspiration." Saturday, the 22nd, would be a national day of protest to End The War In Vietnam. Win Allen decided he was going to organize Harrisonville's first anti-war march, a ragamuffin parade of cowdunged kids screaming anti-imperalist slogans right under the Harrisonville brownshirts' high and mighty noses. On Wednesday, the 19th of April, Win Allen and Ootney Simpson, friendly, grinning, and wary, marched to the office of the city attorney and requested a parade permit. They were told they didn't need one. "We want something in writing, not jive," Win said. "Go ahead and march," the ferret-faced attorney smiled, but he'd give them no papers. Charlie Simpson, who trusted his instincts, was sure it was a trap. "The fuckers'll just bust us," he said.

But Win's dreams escalated. The march would protest not only the war but the new town ordinances. Win would carry a sign that said "DOWN WITH NIXON'S WAR!" and Ootney would carry a sign that said: "DOWN WITH G.M. ALLEN'S WAR!"

"It's gonna be most ricky-tick," Win said.

"Crazy fucking niggers," Charlie laughed.

G.M. Allen heard about the hullabaloo the Nigger and the hippies were planning and went to see Chief Davis about it. He wasn't going to have his weekend spoiled. The Firefighters Association of Missouri would be in town and each of the forty departments was bringing its prize revved-up fire engine. At two o'clock Saturday afternoon, after they finished caucusing over the tornadoes, all those beautiful emery-clothed firetrucks, their sirens blasting, would form a cortege around the square.

All the firefighters would be in their starched parade civvies and the sidewalks would be crammed with gawkward farmers who'd come into town to see the firetrucks and spend a few dollars while they were there. It would be a redlettter day, the biggest hoop-de-doo on the square since those horseshoe-pitching contests they once held. G.M. Allen was damned if he was going to let those spitshined firetrucks be set upon by an army of yammering crablice—hometown purvoids spewing filth, contumely, and treason.

THE day after the cat-and-mouse session with the city attorney was spent coordinating Saturday's anti-war march. Win Allen and Ootney Simpson discussed logistics with their hippie/freak cohorts. They agreed it was a set up, the march certain to end in Sheriff Gough's cockroached jail. But they didn't care. They'd march anyway. Fuck it! They were stagestruck, high on their own grandiose daydreams. The theatrical aspects were too tempting, too ricky-tick to fret about the whip and thud of the brownshirts' axhandle billyclubs. They'd march up Wall Street, gathering at Guido's Pizza minutes before the firefighters assembled near the Missouri Farm Association silo. The square would be decked with bunting and the farmers would be tiptoeing the sidewalks waiting for the sirens when, led by Win Allen, led by a Nigger! the outlaws would stumble into that stars-and-stripes arena, blowing mossgrown minds, ruining everything, pillorying the square with clenched power fists and that eyeteeth-rattling cry: "One! Two! Three! Four! We Don't Want Your Fucking War!"

Word went out Thursday to the timid and sheepish Teeny-Bros at the high school that those interested in going to jail for The Cause should come to the square and Win or Rise or Ootney would give them the info. A lot of kids showed up; the Teeny-Bros themselves were in the process of launching an acned guerilla action of their own, a pep-rally kind of protest against bar b-q ham on cheese bun, chicken fried steak w/ creamgravy, and cheese-burger noodle loaf. The high school lunch menu was not as nutritious as their Nadered palates demanded and the Teeny-Bros were actually threatening to take to the schoolyard if the nutritional quality didn't improve, talking about carrying placards that said: "No More Bar B-Q Ham!" and waving them in front of the dumbstruck principal's office.

The Teeny-Bros were almost as fired up about hair. The *Harrisonville Wildcat News,* concerned in years past with school spirit and jack o' lantern contests, published a sizzling letter to the editor that said: "Upon the start of the fresh school year, a delegation of concerned students met with the principal. We were assured that as long as a certain teacher employed by the junior high school continued to keep his hair at such a length that it doesn't comply with the dress code, we would not be held liable for our hair. The teacher has not cut his hair. Yet three people have been suspended at Harrisonville High School because of hair. What gives? Is it possible for our principal to be lacking in personal integrity to such a degree that he will say one thing and then act in an opposite manner?"

So the Teeny-Bros drifted into town that afternoon, keeping a timorous eye out for the footpatrols—Officers Don Marler and Francis Wirt—and organized themselves into action groups. The freshmen and sophomores—The Snots—would paint signs. The Snots were antpants-anxious to paint words like "No More War!" and show off their militancy. As the day wore on and the footpatrols told Chief Davis there seemed to be a bow-wow of outlaws in town, some of the outlaws got bored and went home, while other part-time badmen slouched by, having heard about Win's Dee-Vine Inspiration from some squiggly-excited Teeny-Bro. Charlie Simpson went home around four o'clock to his Holden roominghouse, going along with Win's fantasy reluctantly, noting the ironies offered by the prospect of the two parades. The firefighters would be cheered because they fought flames; the outlaws would be jailed because they fought war. "Fuck it, they'll just bust us," Ootney told Win Allen again, "the whole shit turns my teeth sour." Ootney was tired. He was going home to mowdown some squirrels with his ittybitty machine gun.

Harry Miller was one of the hangers-on who slouched by— about an hour after Charlie Simpson left to do battle with his doomed squirrels. Harry Miller drove into the square, nodding respectfully at brownshirts Marler and Wirt, and catfooted over to Rise and Win and some of the others. Everything looked cool: Win was chasing dragonflies.

Harry Miller is twenty-four years old and his jeans are too tight; a gut bulges at his belt. His face is puffy and there is a Brando-like sluggishness, a hovering petulance, about him. He doesn't rattle easily and he looks like he can take care of himself. His hair is parted in the middle and shoved to the sides, but it isn't long enough and sometimes a few strands dangle into his forehead forming perfect spitcurls.

It was nearly 5:30. The air was stuffed with heat and they were thirsty. Win, Rise, Gary Hale, Harry Miller, George Russell, and Johnson Thompson, their jiving smart-cracking courtjester, walked across the street to Lloyd Foster's drugstore. One of the Teeny-Bros, whose mother had given him allowance money that morning, was assigned to spend it on a carton of Pepsi-Cola.

"Here we are," Harry Miller says, "standing not exactly under the drugstore's roof but out in front, near the Sears store, which Old Lloyd's boy, Don, runs. So we're waiting for this kid to bring us some bellywash. We are standing right beside a mailbox which is public property. Okay, out of nowhere, Don Foster drives up. Man, I seen that car coming, you could tell he was gonna do something, it was in his eyes, like he already knew he was gonna do this. Okay, when he comes over there, there were already police parked on the other side of the square so we couldn't see 'em. Don Foster pulls up and he immediately jumps out and storms up. He's a big guy, wears nice cowboy boots, got sideburns, carries a pencil behind his ear, walks around wanting to cut down trees.

"So he storms up and he starts saying—'Get away from my store!' He says to Win—'Get your black ass out of here!' So he starts violently throwing shit and John Thompson says—'Listen, man, we pay taxes, I'm not getting out of here.' So the Foster dude says—'Oh, you wanna fight? I'll fight you!' So he pushes John with both hands, just pushes John and knocks him back. John weighs about forty pounds less than the dude and most of his weight is stuck up on top of his head in his hair. Well, right then I caught a sense . . . I knew exactly what was gonna happen. Okay, so then the old man, Lloyd, comes running out and starts throwing some bogus shit. I don't know what he was saying, just yelling and screaming. Somehow Don Foster got ahold of John again and pushed him again.

"So I got in between them. I says to Foster—'Man, leave us alone, you're trying to fight us, you wanna get us throwed in jail, just leave our asses alone, we're not going to jail for you.' And he says—'You get out of the way or I'll smack your ass, buddy!' So I got out of the way and they got off by theirselves again and started piling at it. So his father, Old Lloyd, says—'By Gawd, I'm gonna call the police!' So he walks back to his store, takes about four steps, doesn't even get to his phone, turns back out again watching them hassle, and here comes the police already turning the corner of the courthouse, boogeying from the courthouse. Okay, after they turn the courthouse, it is like fifty feet before the first one gets to the fight—here's John and this Don Foster on the ground.

"The Foster dude is on top smacking John beside the head. John's on the bottom getting ahold of him by the neck and the ear. So here's Sgt. Jim Harris, the police officer, the other two pigs (Officers Don Marler and Francis Wirt) are behind him. Okay, so Harris, five hundred feet away, has his club in the air, running right at him. Here's John on the bottom with Foster on top of him. So Harris twists around and leans down so he can hit John even with Foster on top of him. He hits John in the shoulder and across the side of the face. Foster jumps off and the other two policemen pick up Foster's jacket for him. Foster gets his jacket and walks up beside his old man and Old Lloyd starts pointing at us, saying—'Him! and Him! and Him!' and points to Win and says—'The Nigger! The Nigger! The Nigger!' over and over again. So the pigs put us all under arrest for disturbing the peace and start walking us over to the jail in the sheriff's office. Eight of us: Rise and Win and Gary Hale and John Thompson and George Russell and some of the others.

"On the way over there, one of the pigs decides he's gonna have a little fun with Win. So he sticks Win in the spine with his nightstick as hard as he can. When Win turns around, the pig yells—'The Nigger's resisting arrest!' and when we get to the jail Win gets charged with resisting arrest. When we get to the jail we says—'We wanna file a complaint against the Foster dude for pushing John 'cause, I mean, if they're gonna play that game on you, you might as well play it back on them. Chief Davis is there and the sheriff is there and Sgt. Jim Harris is there and they all said they didn't have the authority for us to file a complaint. So we had to just scream, say—'Goddamnit! I want a damn report! I wanna file a complaint!' I mean we had to scream for fifteen, twenty minutes. I mean scream like maniacs to get them to do it. Finally they brought the city attorney down and he gives us two sheets of paper with nothing on it except the top says 'Municipal Court' and some bogus printed stuff. But all they had us do was sign our names on it and that couldn't—man, when you file a complaint there's something wrote down there and you read it, so that couldn't have been any real complaint form. Okay, so that was just to get us to shut up. They throw us in jail and we knew it was bogus, we just took it as it was, $110 apiece. Then our Nigger, he was about the last one to come in. We hollered across the monkeybars over to his cell and we say—'Hey, Win, how we gonna get out?' And he says—'You know, I don't know, my bail's $1,110.' So that nudge in the back they gave him was to make them a thousand dollars.

"That jail is like the inside of a toilet bowl in a place where everybody's got the backdoor trots, know what I mean? We had to take a shit, well, we had to get a *Look* magazine and tear the pages and put it on the seat it was so grubby. The shitter didn't really have a seat on it—it was a light brown color. They had some drunks over in the bullpen but they didn't want us to have any luxuries. The drunks didn't say nothing to us, nobody said nothing. There were cops crawling out of the ratholes. We must have scared the pricks off of 'em. Here's eight guys in jail, right? They had six highway patrolmen there, they had five guys from the city police department, they had five guys from the sheriff's department, about seven policemen from the surrounding towns in the county."

As long as he lives, Harry Miller says, he will remember the zaniness of that seriocomic night. "All right, here we are, all of us in the crabseat with the whole fucking militia of pigs standing around and looking at us and, man, the front door opens and here comes the game warden! . . . the fucking Cass County game warden carrying a big hunting rifle and he says—'I heard about the trouble, you need any *hep?*' Drunk as a pissass skunk, drunk on whiskey. Right there I just set down and tried to shit my pants for glee but I couldn't."

He almost did, though, when he saw G. M. Allen. "The

Chief of the Fire Department! Yes siree, G. M. Allen, comes in all aflutter. Had this little red firehat on, Number 4. He says to the pigs—'Did you get 'em all? Anybody hurt?' G. M. walks up and down real slow, looking at us, looking us over, looking us in the hair, and then he says—'Where's the Nigger? I got something to say to the Nigger.'"

Win Allen says: "Dig, here I am, under arrest, in the clink. And this dude comes up to me in his little cute firehat and I expect him to say something to me about what happened. So he comes up to me, gets real friendly allasudden, and whispers— 'Win, I want you to come see me tomorrow about that bill you owe me.' He has the fucking *audassity* to come to me in the clink and talk to me about a loan my family owes him."

Harry Miller glanced out the jailwindow as the two Allens, banker and Nigger, talked, and saw one of the town firetrucks loaded with G. M.'s volunteer-firemen. "They were up there in front of the jail standing on the firetruck real stiff, holding fire axes in their hands, actually holding fire-axes."

A sixteen-year-old apple-cheeked high school dropout named Robin Armstrong, misty-blond and honey-cute, a strangely vague and muted farmgirl whose father blew his brains out two years ago —"I'm fed up with everything," she'd say, "people are just so fucking ignorant anymore"—was standing in front of the fire-truck. All of her friends were in jail and she was screaming 'You fucking pigs!' and the firemen were clutching their gleaming hatchets.

Her mother drove up then and Robin Armstrong, trembling with fear and fury, scampered like a panicked jackrabbit down an alley . . . away from her mother, away from G. M. Allen's firemen. "I saw it from the window," Harry Miller says, "Robin starts boogeying in-between the jail and the Retirement Home. She's gonna run down this old road because she don't want her mother to capture her ass. So the firetruck has a tank with two-hundred pounds of pressure in it and you know that big hose they have— well, they open that big hose up and hit Robin in the back with it and knock her to the ground. They skidded her face across the gravel."

The outlaws spent their night in the crabseat wiping their asses with *Look* magazine and organizing their Saturday parade, wondering all the time how they'd make bail. One of their Bros was up all night, making phone calls and drinking whiskey, asking the parents to bail their kids out. He was getting nowhere. They didn't want to spend hard-earned money getting their crybaby kids out of jail. As the sun came up, redeyed Ootney Simpson had figured only one way to get his friends out of the monkeybars.

At 11 o'clock Friday morning, Charlie Simpson, smiling like a dimwit fool, worn to the edge, showed up at the sheriff's office. The outlaw looked the sheriff in the eye and put $1,550 in cash on the counter. It was his life's savings, bankroll for the plot of land he dreamed about. His dream was dead. A sweat of fatigue caked his face.

"Simpson's the name," the dreamer said, "revolution's my game. Free the people!"

THAT didn't go over very well with the sheriff, but Bill Gough didn't say anything about it. Those longhairs were raising yapping hell all morning and driving him stircrazy. It'd be an honest-to-God pleasure to get them out of his jail; he'd take those friendly old juiceheads anyday. It looked like a long weekend cropping, what with the firefighters coming in that night and those crazy hippies still jabbering—right in his jail—about holding their protest march tomorrow.

So he didn't give the Simpson boy any trouble when he said: "Free the people!" in a shade louder voice than the sheriff liked to hear in his office. He counted the stacks of bills, looked up just how much the bond was, and told his deputy to start getting the longhairs out of their cells. Simpson had a big smile pasted to his face, but he looked like he hadn't slept for weeks. The whites of his eyes were more cranberry than white; his hands were skittery. When the Anderson boy walked in, Simpson looked at him like he was going to kill him, and before the sheriff could do anything Simpson had him by the lapels. "Now listen here," Bill Gough said, "you fight in here, both of you are gonna go to jail! I don't care how much money you got."

Rise Risner had just been brought out of his cell and was standing next to the counter when John Anderson came through the door. "Anderson works at TWA with some computers, but he always made out that he was a friend of ours, rapping to us and stuff. Anderson was there the night before, Thursday, when we were being taken to jail. Well, he had enough money on him to get some of us out and he didn't do it. He didn't want to spend his damn money. Ootney found out about it and when he saw Anderson he said—'Look, you fucker, you're supposed to be a friend of ours. I don't want you to ever fuck me over like that! This is nothing personal but you better not ever fuck me over that way.'"

Simpson looked fiddle-faced and strungout to everyone. "He was tired, yeah," Win Allen says, "but it was more. He was pissed off bad. I think the money had a lot to do with it—like, this was the money he was gonna buy his land with, dig, and it had turned into jail money. And he was pissed off about me, too. He told me after he got us out, he said—'Nigger, if your face was as white as my ass, you wouldn't be having all this shit.' He goes—'These fucking crackers, they gonna lynch you up against a tree one night.' Then he laughed. Ootney was like that. He was jolly and jiving but the vibes were like off-center. It was like there was a bomb inside his head."

Standing around the watertower outside the jail, they concluded it was more important than ever to stage their anti-war march. They went to George Russell's house, where Ootney "leaned up against a wall and looked like he was gonna fall asleep."

"You fucking jailbirds kept me up all night!" he said.

"Ootney lost his beauty sleep," they hooted.

Rise says: "We were real determined we had to be in that square the next day marching with those signs and screaming. The bust was the best example of the kind of shit we had all felt. Old Lloyd had just to point his finger and say—'Him! and Him!' and it was enough to send us all to the crabseat."

Win Allen decided they'd hand pamphlets out Saturday as

they marched around the square "so the Truth can be put up on the walls." Hasty essays had to be composed about war, repression, racism, and the new town ordinances.

"Come on, Ootney," Win said. "Help us write some of this shit."

"Okay," Simpson said, "I'll write how much I like fucking."

They raspberried him and threw him lip-smacking mock farts, figuring, as Rise says, "we'd better leave old Ootney alone cause he looked pretty tired." But he brightened after a while, and before the meeting ended, offered to help. A friend of his in Holden had a mimeo-machine and he'd take the essays over there and have them run off.

"Ootney's the production manager!" Rise yelled, and as the others laughed, Simpson came alive, dancing around, his fists flying, shadowboxing Rise's punching-bag belly.

"Come on! Come on!" he yelled, "Charlie Simpson's gonna take on all you creepo fuckers!"

Rise says: "After a while we split up and Ootney took the stuff we wrote up and he was gonna take it over to Holden to the friend of his that had the machine. He asked me if I wanted to go over there with him and I said sure. We piled on into his 1952 Chevy. That was Ootney's batmobile. It was an old, falling-apart car that made a lot of noise. He loved the car, said it was a real hippie car. So we drove on out and we got outside a place called Strasburg and the goddamn car blows up. So we sat there not believing it, you know, here we are and I just got out of jail and Ootney didn't get any sleep and now the goddamn car blows up. Well, we couldn't believe it. We were so pissed off we couldn't do nothing but stand there and mumble and say 'Fuck-It!' and laugh.

"So we decided we were gonna hitch-hike into Holden and then hitch-hike back to Harrisonville. Ootney had his sleeping bag in the back and the M-1 but I didn't think nothing of it 'cause he and I were always going target-shooting with the thing. So he puts the rifle into his sleeping bag and we're standing there hitch-hiking and the car's still smoking. Then this dude from Harrisonville that we know comes along and picks us up. He's going back to Harrisonville, so he drives us back there and we get my car. We drive into Holden and run the shit off with the mimeo-machine and then we had nothing to do. So Ootney says —'Let's just take the gun and shoot some target practice.' We were gonna spend the night out in the woods."

As Charlie Simpson and Rise Risner drove from Holden to Harrisonville late Friday afternoon, they talked. The radio was thumping and Rise only half-listened. The conversation was like a hundred others they'd had. "Nothing much," Rise says, "just a lot of shit, raptalk. Maybe he was trying to tell me something, but if he did, maybe I wasn't listening that close."

They talked about astrology. Ootney was a Pisces and as they speeded past the wheatfields and the greening countryside, he talked to Rise about being a Pisces. He'd read a book that said he'd be nothing but a dreamer all his life and never make any money. The book said a Pisces was "self-destructive."

"So what does that mean?" Rise asked.

"I don't know," Ootney laughed, "maybe it means I'm fucked up."

"Yeah, it means you'll fuck yourself to death," Rise said.

They talked, too, about dope. Ootney said he hadn't done any dope for a while and didn't want to do any "because every-time I smoke a joint I think about how everybody's fucking us over and I get all depressed and down."

As Rise drove into town, he heard Charlie Simpson say a few quiet sentences that stuck in his mind.

"Every time I turn around, I'm getting fucked-up somehow.

Shit, I can't even buy a piece of land when I got the money. It's always the same shit. Ain't it ever gonna stop?"

"When we got into town," Rise says, "we were stopped at the red light and the radio was playing the new Stones song. I was beating on the dash and saying 'Tumbling-tumblin' and all of a sudden Charlie jumps out of the car and runs up the street. He was out of the car and halfway up the street before I even knew what happened. And I freaked right there. What the fuck was he doing? He had the fucking gun. What the fuck was he running up the street for with that fucking gun in his jacket?"

Rise panicked. He made a fast turn, stepped on the gas, and "started boogeying out of Harrisonville, going the other direction."

When Simpson jumped out of the car, Charles Hale, Gary's younger brother, ran to him. He asked Simpson if he'd seen Gary.

"He just shook his head," Charles Hale says, "the only thing I noticed was . . . he had this great big beautiful smile on his face."

Gary Hale was on the other side of the square with Win Allen. "So all of a sudden," Win says, "we heard this Rat!-tat!-tat!-tat!-tat! like. And I said—'Hey, Gary, that sounds like some caps, man,' and he said—'That's what it sounds like to me.' We looked at one another and we got vibes instantly, we said—'Wait a minute, man, who's all here?' So then we see people starting to run and we started boogeying and we heard these two pigs were shot. And then we heard—'There's a dirty hippie down there, dead' and we all, like, we saw Charlie's body . . . and like we couldn't identify with that blood."

Rise drove around for a while, scared, and then, finally, drove back to the square. "By the time I got there the two dead pigs had been taken off the street but Charlie was still laying in the street where he had shot himself, all covered up. All I could see was his boots sticking out from under the plastic bag. My knees kind of buckled and I was leaned up against this building and I just kind of went down. I passed out on the sidewalk and I lay there a few seconds. There's this woman who runs the cleaners and I've known her all my life and she goes—'Well, he tried to shoot me, Johnny' and I didn't say anything.

" 'Why did he try to shoot me, Johnny? I didn't do anything to him' and I just screamed—'Shut up, goddamn you, just shut up!' "

G. M. Allen was about to leave his bank for the day when he saw people running and heard the police sirens. He hurried to the other side of the square, saw the people in front of the Allen Bank and Trust Company, and heard about the two policemen killed and the Simpson boy in the alley with his head blown off. He wasn't surprised. He'd expected something like this all along. He felt it in his bones. He turned and headed back to his office as fast as he could. He had to activate the Civil Defense sirens and get on the citizens' band and tell his men to get into town. Gary Hale saw him rushing across the square and went up to him.

"You satisfied now?" Gary Hale said, "you see what you've done?"

"Get out of my way, you little bastard!" G. M. Allen said.

He got to his office and as he pushed the button and the sirens started howling G. M. Allen had a comforting thought.

It was six o'clock; the firefighters coming for their convention would be checking into their motels. He'd have more than enough manpower in Harrisonville that night to handle whatever would happen. Five hundred firefighters from all across the State of Missouri. And right then G. M. Allen said a prayer. He thanked the Lord for giving him the wisdom to plan the convention for the perfect time . . . "when the hippies started doing their killing."

Sirens wailed; the revolution had come to Harrisonville.

Blood was flowing on Pearl Street, and the blueprint was right there, in that day's issue of the high school newspaper, *The Wildcat News*. G. M. Allen read the words and waited for his CD volunteers and visiting firefighters to flock into town. On the day of the cataclysm, almost as if it was timed, *The Wildcat News* was skypuffing a book called *Revolution for the Hell of It* by Abbie Hoffman.

"This book is almost beyond my description. The fantastic account of the demonstrations in Chicago during the 1968 Democratic Convention, their prelude, aftermath, and many other interesting things concerning THE REVOLUTION! It offers some near brilliant insights into what is actually happening in the streets. The book itself is pure Hoffman, free, nonconforming, very unique. He expresses his thoughts exactly as they come to him, without regard to persuasive power or censorship. Most readers will benefit from the ideas and suggestions promoted in this book."

Godalmighty! He was in his hometown, the place he loved, and people he did business with were getting shot down on the square and Abbie Hoffman was getting their own kids' endorsement!

He thought of the policemen killed . . . Marler was a friendly sort, easy to smile, nice family . . . and his eyes got stuck on some of the words in *The Wildcat News:*

"brilliant . . . fantastic . . . THE REVOLUTION! . . . persuasive power . . . ideas . . . suggestions."

FIREFIGHTERS watchdogged the street-corners that night with hatchets and shotguns in their hands. The square was barricaded; police cruisers patrolled the streets leading into town. A riflleman armed with a carbine very much like Charlie Simpson's perched in the courthouse belltower, which commands an overview and a clear shot to every cranny of the square. Around eleven o'clock a thunderstorm rolled in with its gnarled bolts of field-lightning; rain sent the gunmen scurrying to their cars.

About an hour after the shooting, Win Allen was walking across the square and a policeman told him: "You got two of ours, now it's time we get some of you!"

When a curfew was announced that night, Win and Rise and their Bros hustled out of town and decided to stay out. "There was blood in those people's eyes," Rise says. "It was like we'd all pulled that trigger, not just Ootney. They couldn't do anything to Ootney because he was smart and blew his brains out, but we were still there. I was really scared. Those people were crazy. The pigs were looking at us like they could hardly wait to tickle their triggers. We knew that if any of us, like, made the smallest wrong move, one of us would be dead and they'd just make up some bogosity and get away with calling it justifiable murder."

G. M. Allen says: "I was just happy we had all those men

in town. Besides that, we had policemen come from as far as fifty miles away. We didn't know what to expect, but we were ready. We thought some of the hippies might wanna shoot some more policemen or some innocent people. It didn't make sense, not any of it, unless you figure the whole thing was planned and Simpson was talked into killing those policemen for the sake of their revolution."

On Saturday, April 22nd, the national day of protest to end the War in Vietnam, the curfew was lifted—but only during the day, until six o'clock that night. A few of the firefighters and policemen got some shuteye, but gunmen still guarded the square and a rifleman still stood in the belltower, using binoculars to scan the alleys and the rooftops. Harrisonville's first anti-war protest was canceled, and after only brief debate, the firefighters decided to call off their parade.

"You mean we drove those trucks all the way out here for nothing?" a firefighter asked G. M. Allen.

"It ain't fair, sure," G. M. Allen said. "But I figure a lot of people are gonna be too scared to come into town."

He was dead wrong. Except for the longhairs, everyone within a hundred miles seemed to drive into Harrisonville that day. Traffic was backed up for half a mile, all the way to the FINA gas station, and people stood with Kodak Brownies around the spots which had been pools of blood the day before.

In the course of florid description, rumor fed upon rumor and, after a while, reality itself seemed a figment of the imagination . . . The Simpson boy had eaten a plateful of LSD just before he did the killing . . . The gun was traced to the Black Panther Party in Chicago . . . Simpson belonged to a Communist hippie group in Kansas City . . . They found some dynamite in the MFA silo . . . Two longhairs were heard shouting "The revolution's on!" . . . The hippies had decided to kill the whole town, like Charlie Manson had killed those people in California . . . The courthouse would be burned that night . . . The hippies had a list of townspeople who were going to get killed . . . The National Guard was coming in.

And the pickup trucks carrying whole families who hardly ever came to town kept roaring in on this day. Excited rubbernecking little kids stood by the Retirement Home's gray walls and asked: "Is this where he killed hisself, Mommy?"

Saturday night, the gunman in the belltower saw something move on the roof of the Harrisonville Hotel. He yelled to the firefighters across the street and, within minutes, the hotel was surrounded by dozens of men carrying all sorts of weapons—from Colt .45s to mailorder Lee Harvey Oswald specials.

"Give yourself up!" a deputy's bullhorn echoed. "You're surrounded!"

There was a crash on the pavement and an old wino who'd found a comfortable spot for the night yelled: "Don't shoot, don't shoot, I'm coming" and miraculously no shots were fired. The old drunk had dropped his pint of whiskey from the rooftop in shitpants fear. A deputy was assigned to sweep the glass off the street.

The burials were held Monday. Patrolman Don Marler's was the first. More than five hundred policemen came to the funeral, many of them from Kansas City. Marler's open casket was in the church foyer but was banged shut minutes before his wife and family got there. The minister said: "The fact that everyone dies is proof that all have sinned. But God says it does not end there. Our friend took the shortcut home." The city council held a meeting before Marler's funeral and voted to pay for the funerals of both policemen. A reporter asked if the curfew would be extended and Mayor M. O. Raine, the magisterial tooth-jumper, said: "This is a black day. I don't like to have too many decisions made when people are so emotional. So I'm not gonna make that decision now."

Charlie Simpson was buried last—in Chilhowee, a tiny town

not far from Holden, in the cemetery where his grandparents are buried. Rise Risner, who was one of the pallbearers, says: "There was a whole lot of people there. I think about half of 'em were pigs because a lot of 'em had cameras. This dude, this minister, like you could tell he wasn't too happy about having to bury Ootney. He was just going through the motions, like he was the one who got stuck with burying a sack of shit. The minister was talking about how Jesus died and all this shit and he didn't say one fucking thing about Charlie. They didn't have anything at all about him; they didn't say one fucking thing about his life. Nothing. He was rapping all this shit about fucking burying Jesus and 'He rose' and all this shit. I thought he was talking about Charlie for a long time until I figured out what he was talking about. At the end, John Thompson sang 'Blowin' in the Wind' and we all chimed in."

After the ceremony, as they were bringing the casket out of the church in the glare of the television cameras and wire service photographers, the pallbearers clenched their fists and held them to the sky, their other hand on the plain wooden box with Charlie Simpson's rouged suit-dressed corpse in it. "We gave the power fist 'cause we figured that would be a way of showing everybody that Ootney was a brother," Rise says. "No matter what kind of shit they were saying about him. He was one of us. We did it 'cause we loved him."

Some of the townspeople saw and others heard about the pallbearers' fists and, at first, no one knew what to make of it. But then G. M. Allen told Mayor Raine he heard it meant someone else was going to die. Mayor Raine told some of the aldermen and by nightfall the word was out all over town: The hippies were going to kill another policeman! So the curfew was extended still another day and the rifleman stayed chainsmoking and cooped-up in his belltower.

The curfew was lifted, finally, the next day, but Win Allen and Rise Risner and Gary Hale and their Bros still didn't feel safe going into town. They drove to the City Park, a mile from town, and were surrounded by guns within minutes.

"You gonna get your asses outta here," a policeman told Rise, "or we gonna get even!"

Feelings of wildeyed hate and vengeance reached such pitch that Win and Rise collected their Bros and left town, camping out in an open and nearly inaccessible field six miles away. "I was afraid they'd come to one of our houses like one of those lynching parties on TV and just take us," Rise says. "It was cold out there and it rained and we were wet as hell . . . but we were alive." By Friday, feelings were so red-raw ugly that the Rev. W. T. Niermeier, who'd preached at patrolman Marler's funeral, wrote a column in the *Democrat-Missourian* that said: "A word of God for our community at this time. Recompense to no man evil for evil. Live peaceably with all men. Dearly beloved, avenge not yourselves. Thou shalt not follow a multitude to do evil."

That day's *Democrat-Missourian* carried a news story about the shooting but nothing about the circumstances. "Well, I didn't want to write too much about Simpson," said J. W. Brown, editor-publisher, "not after all the trouble he caused us. I figured folks just wouldn't want to read about him and if folks don't want to read about something, I don't print it." He pointed proudly to his newspaper's accomplishments. That same year, the *Democrat-Missourian* was awarded its sixteenth Blue Ribbon Weekly Newspaper citation by the Missouri Press Association—for "outstanding performance in the field of journalism."

The next issue of the paper carried a two-column ad, partly the result of the funerals J. W. Brown had to attend that week. He talked to some of the directors and they determined the funeral homes didn't do enough advertising in his newspaper and, the next week, the bold black-bordered ad, which in a ghoulish way Charlie Simpson had solicited, said:

A HOUSE WITHOUT A WOMAN
is like a body without soul or spirit. Benjamin Franklin's words of wisdom recognize that a house becomes a home through the loving touch of a woman and the warm glow of a friendly hearth. Likewise, we believe, a funeral director becomes more than a business man since his prime object is to be of service to those in need. It is with humble pride that we serve the citizens of this community.

Friday afternoon, a week after the shooting, G. M. Allen was talking to one of his customers about the list the hippies were supposed to have of the people they were going to kill. G. M. said he heard he was Number One on that list. "I don't hold too much by it," G. M. Allen said, "maybe there isn't even any list—but, by God, they try something—well, I was in the Infantry during the War, they better think about that!"

A few days after that, Luke Scavuzzo, who runs Scavuzzo's Grocery and is an alderman, appeared on a television talk show in Kansas City and said: "Maybe some people in town pushed those kids too much." Now, Luke Scavuzzo said, "Some people have learned they better *ease up.*" By nightfall, town scuttlebutt held that Luke Scavuzzo was saying they were going to *"give up."* The next day some people told Luke Scavuzzo they weren't going to buy his groceries anymore because he was *yellah.*

"Luke had to go around for a whole week telling everybody he never said that," G. M. Allen says. "He should have known better. Nobody's gonna give up or ease up. Are we supposed to wait around till someone else gets killed?"

A few weeks after Charlie Simpson turned the town square into a free-fire zone, the Civil Defense sirens yowled again and people ran to their citizens' bands expecting to hear their fears confirmed. More trouble! Another killing! The voice of G. M. Allen was as breathless and garbled as the last time. But this time there was less to worry about. It came out of the east and overturned a mobile home, knocked down some outhouses, and then it was gone.

Just another miserable goddamn tornado.

THE first person I saw when I drove into town was Win Allen. He was lying on the courthouse steps, pressed flat with his face to the cement. He didn't move and he stayed that way, as still as the pennies on a deadman's eyes, for what seemed like a long time. I got there about two weeks after the shooting; by that time Win and Rise and their Bros had decided it was safe enough to go back into town. The old mock-heroic game for the town square would go on. Four fresh graves weren't going to get in the way.

I got out of the car and walked into the drugstore for a pack of Luckies. An old man behind the counter was staring out the window at Win Allen. He watched me get out of the car. His eyes must have picked out the Missouri plates because when I walked in his tone was conspiratorial and trusting. "See that nigger boy up there?" Lloyd Foster said. "He's been climbing those steps every day for four days now and just laying down there. He goes up there and he looks around and he puts his fist up in the air and then he lays down on top of his face. He pretends he's dead. They say it's a way of remembering the crazy hippie that killed our policemen."

I was wearing a regimental Polo tie and navy blue blazer and the next few days I wore the same getup, exaggerating the effect, walking around with a fat Special Corona 77 cigar sticking out of my teeth. I sought folks out in the most razorbacked bars in town, buying them Bud and Colt malt liquor and getting them to talk. I slicked my hair back above my ears and bought a bottle of gooky hair-oil. With cigar, coat, and tie, I must have looked respectable enough: pretty soon they were buying me beers. I told them I was from a magazine in San Francisco and forgot to say which one. I think the cigar and the greasy hair got me through. When I got back to the motel at night and looked in the mirror, I saw a guy I remembered from somewhere . . . but I couldn't place him.

When I finished talking to the townspeople, I drove back to my motel, shampooed my hair, and changed. I put my jeans on, let my hair fall down over my ears, wore my cowhide jacket, and drove back into town. I was getting pretty tired of cigars anyway. I found Win Allen, told him I was from *Rolling Stone,* and said I wanted to talk about Charlie Simpson. Win Allen almost cried he was so happy. "Man," Win said, "we been watching you watching us and we figured you was FBI. With that cee-gar." We laughed.

That night we gathered around the square—one of the cops I'd talked to spotted me and gave me a fixed evileye—and drove ten miles out of town into the middle of a wheatfield. The car got stuck trying to hump a half-dead creek; we got out and pushed it across. We found a clearing that suited us and built a bonfire. It was a cloudy spring night, about seventy degrees, and the lightning was already playing meaningless patterns off to the east. There were about a dozen of us; we had eight or nine bottles of redwine and a dozen sixpacks of beer.

The fire was roaring blue flames and Rise Risner's red Volkswagen, which had been pulled as close as possible, played Dylan, Hendrix, and, strangely, José Feliciano. We sat around the fire, wished J. Edgar Hoover a speedy trip to hell, drank wine, and talked about Charlie Simpson. The people here were Charlie Simpson's best friends. The setting was peaceful, mellow, and warm . . . and we were talking about a man who'd killed three innocent people in cold blood. They were calling him a brother and telling me how much he loved his fellow man and believed in The Cause.

"Sometimes Ootney said he thought violence was the only kind of revolution there was," Rise said. "But dig," Win said, "as far as a violent revolution—anytime someone infringes on me and fucks me, it makes me mad. That's the way Charlie was thinking, too."

"A lot of freaks you meet in places," Rise said, "somebody will rip them off or something and they'll walk away. Somebody will beat the shit out of them or something and they'll haul ass. But we're not that way. We're country boys. We're willing to fight the motherfuckers if they wanna fight us.

"Ootney was smart," Rise said, "he killed himself to keep the pigs from having the satisfaction of killing him or locking him up in some honky jail. He was into so much cosmic shit, man. He was so heavy with that, it was a religion to him. Like some religions say self-destruction is the best thing you can do for your God, that's why they burn themselves. I know Ootney had to feel the same thing."

"One time Ootney was in a black neighborhood," Win said, "and somebody said something about Jesus to him and Ootney said—'The only way Jesus and I differ is that he was willing to die for the people around him and I'm not ready for that yet.' "

"I think he was Jesus," Rise said. "As far as I'm concerned he was Jesus."

"Because that cat just laid down the truth, man," Win said, "everything that came out of his mouth was truth and supposedly like Jesus laid down the same thing. And when he got up the stuff to die for The Cause, Charlie became of the same instance. He was groovy, outtasight. He had so much compassion for people, sentimental about a lot of things, sensitive."

It'd been an exhausting few days. I'd scrutinized too many vivid details of four vicious killings and something in my mind flailed out now . . . Jesus Simpson, murderer, coldblooded killer, compassionate, sensitive, sentimental. It could've been the fatigue, or the beer chased with wine, but I saw too many grotesqueries running amok in that blaze.

"As far as I'm concerned," Rise said, "Charlie isn't dead. It is just something Charlie wanted to do and if Charlie wanted to do it, I can't say anything about it."

"Yeah," I said, "but what about the people killed and their wives and kids? Don't you care about that?"

"Well, you know," Rise said, "how can I criticize it? It's Charlie's thing. Like it was a far-out thing to do."

We were gathered around this bonfire on a spring night in Missouri and the date was the 4th of May. I'd never had much luck with the 4th of May. My mind lashed back to the past few years . . . On this day in 1971, I was standing around a green field at Kent State University in Ohio listening to requiems and eulogies . . . And on this day in 1970 I was running dazedly around those same lovely fields looking at puddles of blood and asking National Guardsmen why they'd killed four innocent kids.

And now I was talking to some kids asking them why one of their best friends killed three innocent people with the same kind of gun the Guardsmen'd used and all they could say to me was: "Like it was a far-out thing to do."

I told them the story of the May 4ths and Win Allen said: "Dig it, man now it's four to three."

"Right on!" Rise said.

"Old Ootney," Win said, "Old Ootney. That gun was outtasight, man. Like the first time I went to his crib I saw it and I said—'Ootney, is that yours?' and he said—'Yeah, a friend of mine gave it to me' and I said—'Wow, man, sometime when you and I go fishing and out in the woods, maybe I can dig on it.' Like Charles had this big Buck knife with a holster on it and this most beautiful ricky-tick fishing pole and he said—he said whenever he went home, he fondled the stuff all the time, felt it up and dug it."

"Yeah," Rise said, "Ootney loved nature."

My eyes were sucked in by the flames, trapped by ironies and contradictions, watching the wood pop and the smoke drift across the field. It was nearly dawn, my mouth had a burned-out taste, and I was very cold.

Framed by flames, I saw Charlie Simpson dancing inside the fire, fondling his M-1 and his fishing rod. I saw him playing with that warhero gun, talking about loving life and nature. "He was Jesus," Rise had said. I could see Jesus Simpson in his faded bloodstained bluejeans smiling beatifically, squeezing the trigger, and flashing the peace sign.

I sat redeyed and shivering on a hoarfrosted log and told Win and Rise and their Bros about the things I'd seen crackling at me in their cursed fire.

"Man," Win said, "that's far-out!"

"Far-out," I mumbled. "Far-out. What the fuck is wrong with us? Is that all we can say?"

Win looked at me funny for a split second and said something. He said it in his own lunatic blackevil language and pointed to a bottle of redwine at my feet.

"Pass the blood," Win said.

II
Ootney

THE telephone was his first kill, before the target-practice squirrels and the bleeding men on the square. He took it to the wooded slope of a hill outside Harrisonville, a place called Ament Mound, and tied it around the branches of a buckled bastard oak. The receiver fluttered like a gallows-bloated tongue above the ground, which was once an Osage-Shawnee burial mound.

It was a crisp blackberry winter day, his high school sidekick, Harelip Runnels, remembers. On the way out there, dragging the set after him on the ground, Charlie laughed in that goslin giggle of his and said: "It's what she deserves." He took a final honeying glance at her, swaying obscenely off the oak, measured a deadeye twenty steps, and took the old goosegun out of a bunch of rain-yellowed newspapers. He loaded it up with buckshot, took scrutinous sight, and fired. Harelip said: "Now what's the sense of this, Charlie, hear? What you doing this for?" The first shot missed, grazing off some treebark. The second blasted the set apart with a whacking crash, raining the burial mound with broken black metal.

Harelip said: "Boy, are they gonna be mad! You can't go and take something like a telephone."

"They got too many of 'em to notice." Charlie said. "Here, you want a shot?"

Sucking too much wind to say no, Harelip knelt down and

aimed the gun. He fired and missed. Charlie took it back from him with a grump, raised the barrel, and blew the receiver off the treelimb into shrapnel-like pieces.

He crawled around the bastard oak with a burlap potato sack, tenderly dropping each mallyhacked piece into the bag. He took it home and put it in a drawer. The sack with the dead telephone inside it would be one of his lifelong goodluck charms, along with the black Boy Scout knife they found in his pocket when he blew the top of his head off on the square.

He always hated telephones, hated them till his murderous dying day, and when he kidded his buddies and said he'd shot a few phones in his time, no one knew or suspected about the day on Ament Mound when, at the age of sixteen, he gunned down his first victim.

It started many years before then, though, when he was eight or nine years old. The telephone repairman came to the farm two or three times a month because the Simpsons never seemed to be getting their phonecalls. Some crony inevitably saw the old man in town and said: "I tried to call you the last couple days but I guess you folks weren't in." When it kept happening, the repairman came grumbling out, checked the receiver, the set, and the bellbox, and found nothing wrong. It was the most confounded mussel-headed telephone! They could make their calls and nothing was wrong; the dialtone was humming and the operator's voice was uppity and impatient. But when someone called them back the contraption wouldn't work. The repairman was called once when Charlie was still in school and he attacked this hoodooed telephone again. He took everything apart, and there, in the bellbox, between the thin steel rectangular strips that make a phone ring, he found—a dime. It was tucked neatly inside and had the effect of gagging the bellbox. The repairman looked closer and found the screw had been tinkered with; when Charlie got home the old man whipped the unholiness out of him.

Later on, when he was in high school, he and Harelip Runnels and their friends sat around in a wheatfield swilling brusharbor whiskey. Then, of course, nobody knew what to do next
. . . now that they were blind-bear-in-a-cave drunk and it was still early. Charlie said: "Let's go for a ride." They took a bone-rattling Packard reassembled into muffler-banging shape at the Holden junkyard, and Charlie told Harelip to stop whenever he saw a phonebooth. He took each booth at a dead run, whipping out his Boy Scout knife, and chopped and sawed at the cord until the receiver was his. Like some crazed shot-putter, he hurled the receiver as far and as high as he could into the trees. They made seven or eight harebrained stops that night.

When Charlie was up there lolling on the square with Win and Rise and their Bros many years later, he told them never to call him because the telephone was the Bingbuffer's own convenience (the Bingbuffer being a fire-eating demon of the Prairie). The telephone stopped people from really talking to each other, got in the way of man-to-man communication. When Charlie had something to say, Rise noticed, he always said it face-to-face, sometimes driving all those chuckholed miles from Holden to Harrisonville to say something like: "Hey, man, let's go fire-fishing tomorrow night." They didn't quite understand it, though Rise and Win admired the sheer humanism of his craziness.

Piefaced John Runnels, who works in construction these days and wouldn't have any truck with the hippie-boogers on the square, remembers how Charlie told of finding his first kill on the high school principal's desk. Charlie broke a window in the principal's office one night, cooned in, stumbled through the darkness, grabbed the telephone, gave it a smiling vicious tug, and ripped it from the wall.

EMMET the emmet was his first love. Charlie
played for days with each big black ant, keeping it babbling
company, watching it shuckle to and from in frenzied circles on
the farmhouse floor. Then, with doting care, he'd let it crawl onto
a matchbook and Emmet walked the plank back inside the bottle.
He had about a dozen emmets in all and he mothered each of
them five or six days until, no longer able to endure life inside the
medicine bottle, Emmet died.

When Emmet died he took the bottle to the woodshed and
placed it alongside the other bottles, each of which contained
another dead Emmet. Back into the fields he went, hunting
another doomed playmate. He was bedazzled by the fat tarbarrel
bugs and kept the latest bottle, containing its latest captive, by
his bed. He woke up in the morning and hunkered down on the
floor with it, frolicking along as Emmet took his desperate morning dash down the prison floor.

One night Emmet fled an aspirin bottle, crawled onto the
bed, then onto the boy's face. It stung him about the nose and
eyes and left swollen and painful pumpknots. That was the last
Emmet. The boy went back to the shed, picked up the bottles of
dead Emmets, and drained the corpses into a jar. He took the jar
into the yard, poured gasoline over the dead ants, and struck a
match. His Emmets blazed in a barnyard funeral pyre. He went
back inside the house and told the old man he had burned all his

dead Emmets. It was his fault, he said: If he wouldn't have been so kind, if the airhole wouldn't have been as big, then Emmet couldn't have escaped to sting pumpknots into his face.

He fell in love with the yellow-bellied woodpecker the way he had loved his emmets. There were a lot of woodpeckers and sapsuckers around: the redbellies were there all through the year, but the yellow-belly only passed through a few weeks in winter. The old man fashioned him a slingshot—a "Niggershooter"— and he spent bone-cold hours lurking in ambush, waiting for a yellow-belly to swoop down within range. He never managed to bag one. For years afterward, though, he told his friends a horn-swoggling lie. He woke up one morning, he said, hearing a sap-sucker outside. He looked out the window and saw it was a yellow-belly. He called for the bird and it flew right over to him. He patted the bird and could have trapped it but decided to let it go . . . because nobody had a right to trap a bird. Sometimes he would change the story so it took place at night and the yellow-belly turned into a hooting screechowl.

He was born with "bronikal trouble," a severe asthmatic condition which sometimes swelled his nose and throat and blocked his breathing. He never let it interfere with his farm-chores. He loved the soil, this fickle blackland that came from limestone and shale. Rattle-breathing and redfaced, he stayed out in the fields plowing and building haystacks.

Even though he loved the soil righteously, the old man cautioned him, even though the blackland was one of the Lord's biggest gifts to man, he couldn't get himself sick over it.

"I ain't sick," Charlie said, "you can't get sick out there."

Sometimes he went into the fields, found a stretch of clover or cowpeas, and daydreamed the hours away. He came back talking about wolfpacks, bald eagles, and gowrow lizards he had never seen.

He didn't do well in school. He couldn't concentrate on his books and gazed out the window at the land in private guarded reverie. He hotfooted home each day and amused himself with his emmets, sapsuckers, and his blackland. He missed school often, because of boredom and asthma, and played hookey whenever he felt the need. He walked down the road toward the bus-stop, his books in hand, waved to the old man, and doubled back, halfhamming fences. He lazed in the fields, went home when he saw saw the school bus, invented things he didn't do that day, and waited for his whipping.

"How come you don't like school?" the old man asked him.

"Can't learn nothing there," he said.

"What can you learn sitting out there?"

"All kinds of stuff," he said.

Later, when he was in high school, an English teacher tried to teach him about Shakespeare. He wasn't interested in Shakespeare. She was a bony maple-headed spinster who tried to hurt the boy into learning by making fun of him in class. She called him a "dumb peckerwood." He never said anything to her there, but followed her after school. He came out of a thicket, running full burst, and tackled her into a ditch. It raised a lot of sand: he was thrown out of school.

When he was ten years old, he trembled for days. On a spring night, a tornado ripped down from Kansas City. It plucked the heads from the stalks, shaped itself into a swirling matting, and roughed up a part of the farmhouse roof. For a time afterward, whenever the sky turned ocher or crocus and the wind was like dog's breath, he refused to leave the house. In a narrow corner of the cellar, the boy built a crude shelter he called his "Fraid Hole." Whenever the faintest threat of a twister hovered over the blackland, he bellied in there and cowered.

HE choked and puked for breath, but brandishing his umbrella stick, he was Cole Younger taken to the brush. Cole Younger: foraging for food, stealing corn from the cribs, yamping puffed-up hens which never even squawked. He killed, but never in vain, always in virtuousness or self-defense. He raised the umbrella stick to his shoulder, drilling the hapless Harelip, whom he armtwisted into playing the Yankee.

The legacy of Cole Younger, outlaw, Confederate bushwhacker, murderer, rainbowed over the prairie, reified in stories the old man and everybody in town was forever telling. Cole as Robin Hood, giving burned-out Civil War folks free food, riding with Billy Quantrill and later with Jesse James, reckoning with Yankee rapists and barnburners and then with Yankee bankers and money. A woman in Peculiar, an antique dealer, even launched a campaign to holywater Cole's trail. She urged gas-station owners along the highway to hang heavy wooden slats on their doors that said: "This Is Cole Younger Country."

So Charlie, listening to the yarns at the kitchen table and in school (most of the post-Civil War outlaws were born within thirty miles of Kansas City) became Cole Younger. He used the umbrella stick to effect barnyard justice, re-creating scenes of carnage and devastation among the scarlet lobelia which bloomed there.

Harelip Runnels was the Yankee captain; a little girl named

Mary Lander was Belle Starr, Cole Younger's girlfriend, born down the road in Carthage; Skeet Jenkins, who had pockmarks over his face and Vaselined red hair, was the notorious Jesse James.

They playacted one carnal historic moment more than any other: Mary Lander was Cole's virginal little sister, abducted from a dance by the sexfiend Yankee captain. Harelip forced her to the ground, crawdadded on top of her, and as Mary Lander screamed, slapped her gently on the cheek. This was rape. Jesse James, hearing her caterwauling, came racing from the barn as vicious Harelip fled across the fields. Jesse carried her to the hayloft, where Cole's sister told him the Yankee captain had violated her. Cole grabbed his umbrella stick, Jesse James hoisted a musket-shaped treelimb, and the two set off across the fields, riding imaginary palominos, leaving Mary sobbing as they sought to avenge her honor.

Harelip knew the fences and fields and could shimmy a magnolia or black locust in nothing flat. The chase lasted three or four hours, sometimes, climaxing in inevitable ritual murder. Cole and Jesse James found the lust-driven Yankee Harelip, who groveled for mercy. With Jesse holding him, Cole Younger let the umbrella stick fire and shivered bullets into Harelip's degenerate body.

And Jesse always asked, standing over the dying Harelip: "Why didn't you give him a chance?"

And Cole always answered, in the phrase he heard recounted at the kitchen table and found in his history books: "You don't give a mad dog a chance!"

And Harelip said: "Can I get up now?"

Sometimes, when Belle and Jesse James and Harelip didn't cast him company, he went to the brush alone with his umbrella stick and palomino. Yankee manhunts were closing in on him and he hid-out in hollowed treetrunks taking potshots at make-believe posses.

The old man didn't like booing up anything, so he told Charlie about Cole Younger as he really lived: The Great Hero, captured and imprisoned for a bank robbery, in prison twenty-five years; then, free and semisenile, wandering into a revival tent, finding pokeweed religion and becoming a white-haired cocklebur saint preaching the evils of devil-whiskey. But Charlie didn't care much about that. He wanted to hear about Belle, Jesse James, and the firebug Yankees.

One day, when he was playing other games, he and Rise and some of their Bro desperadoes drove to the cemetery in Lee's Summit, twenty miles from Harrisonville, where Cole Younger is buried. They traipsed up and down the graves until they found Cole's stone.

They sat and drank three sixpacks of beer. Charlie told the stories about Belle, the rape, and the Yankee captain. He piled the beercans in a pyramid on Cole Younger's stone and stretched out on the earth alongside it. A cruiser pulled up, its bubble-gum spinning. The cop told the hippies a cemetery was a reverential place . . . unless they had something better in mind than putting beercans on a person's grave, they had no business there.

Cole Younger, who'd discarded his umbrella stick, got up off Cole Younger's grave, looked at the cop—red light spinning behind him—and laughed.

THE junkyard is an island in a mudpool off highway 131, east of the Holden limit, a country mile from the Baptist Temple and the produce company with the checkerboard Purina Chow poster above its clapboard. Dead cars squat and sprawl in steel-twisted stances: belly-up with their innards showing, rusted petticoats anchored to the gravel. Right across the twolane, where a hearse leans with axles to the sky, aberdeen angus mosey in a patch by a barbed-wire fence. On the side of it plops a burnt-orange sofa left for the rubbish truck. A few miles west, an olive-green oil barrel says: "Keep America Beautiful."

Charlie came to the yard with his little brother, Bub, once Charlie stopped hazing him all the time. It was a goldmine of googaws like winged-coon spotlights and small round dirt-encrusted babymoon hubcaps. He and Bub got to be rod artists, able, say, after major surgery, to nurse a totaled '57 Chevy back to supercharged life. They rebuilt cars with collected junk and took artisan's pride in the black lacquer finish and the metalwork. They molded fenders to the body, cut cylinder heads, opened valve pockets, chopped-up the roof, and created thumping hoo-hooer Funny Cars.

It began when the hardhats from Kansas City were fixing chugs in the Interstate and traffic was detoured through Holden. They watched a 24-hour procession of out-of-state cars. At first they wrote down license plates, keeping score on California and

New York. After a while it got to be more fun to sharpeye the cars themselves, and one day they gawked transfixed at a 1947 Ford coupe, mean and gleaming with godlike chrome, chopped, channeled, flare-fendered.

Inspired, Charlie began treasure-hunting at the junkyard, making special trips the day after some donked-up fool bit a curve and wound up sky-goggling in an apple-orchard. He examined the new casualty, sometimes wiping fresh-dried blood off the knife-glass in the windshield, and bided his time. His diagnosis told him which body parts could be transplanted onto his own machine. If the blood-slobbered car was left for dead, he took his tools to the yard and went to work. He had some needlenose pliers, a ball-peen hammer, a ratcheting box wrench, a slothead screwdriver, and a dozen other auto-surgical instruments. He was able to transplant his treasures within minutes.

He hung out at places like Gary's Drive-In in Chilhowee, past the intersection of the only Route o in the state, known as the road to nowhere. It is a truckstop, one of the places drivers call a heartburn palace. He sat by the counter, shooting the shit with a waitress who more often than not wore a fresh black eye, and waited for the truckers to beach their semis and stagger in for transfusions of greenhot coffee.

He said he wanted to be just like them. Punchy, maybe needing company to stay awake, they fed him the lore of the berm and the center-strip. He went back to Bub and the old man and twaddled about tailgate racers who stretched it all out and concrete-eating barebacks that galloped the road because their wheels weren't balanced.

"I asked this trucker to lift his hood," he said once, "and he said he'd lift it if I zipped my fly down."

"What did you do?" the old man asked him.

"I zipped it down and he looked at my pecker."

"Did he hurt you?"

"Naw, he felt it and I said—'How about it, mister? A deal's a deal' and he told me to zip it up and lifted his hood."

One afternoon he drove off and didn't come back. When he finally got back the next morning, gunning his cowpatch dragster into the drive, he was good-hearted and happy. He'd slept like a civvy cat out at the junkyard. He was hunting a mirror and it started to drizzle. He got tired, crawled into a dead mildewed taxi, and woke up with the fieldmice scuttling the hood of the cab.

He burned out a series of cars, driving each of them until they fell apart or until he could find no more parts at the yard, and it was during this time he first hitched horns with Al Wakeman, the police chief of Holden.

Applesauce Wakeman is a backslapping voluble man who relishes the sound of his own voice. He has but two men on his force and is often out in the streets himself, looking for revenue-sharing speeders, stopping by at Dorothy's Cafe and Lloyd's IGA Foodlane to socialize and sip coffee.

Everytime Applesauce Wakeman drove down 131 in his bran-spanking new cruiser, he ran into Charlie or Bub Simpson racing some new falling-apart noisemaker. The noisemakers were equipped with bald out-of-size suicide tires. A lot of people were complaining about these Simpsons, who seemed to think 131 was their own board and dirt racetrack. Applesauce pulled them over whenever he heard their jalopies go ear-bursting by.

"You're always stopping us," Charlie said, "you're picking on us."

"You can't go beating around without a muffler. It's disturbing the peace."

"But there ain't any mufflers at the yard."

"Then pay your fine," Applesauce said, "and get off the road."

Applesauce Wakeman cited Charlie Simpson half a dozen times. He never figured 131 would lead him one spring day to Gary's Drive-In where, surrounded by truckers gulping Benzedrine chasers, the police chief talked to the eye-blackened waitress about the traffic jam outside.

Charlie Simpson was a few hundred feet away, in the company of respectable people named Levi Evans and Leonardus Askew, across the street from Wharton's Grocery Store, where a scrawl of whitewash on red brick said: "Jane for homecoming queen." Applesauce Wakeman directed traffic as Charlie Simpson lay streteched out on his back, around the corner from his favorite heartburn palace, on a strip of flatland backdropped by outhouses and ewe-necked mules. A minister funeralized over his coffin and all the tiny town's eyes were glued on the windy old boneyard.

FLAMES followed him to sleep, torchlighted his dreams. When he woke in the morning, spraying phlegm and mucus, he talked to the old man about the blowtorch in his brain.

He didn't finish high school, devoid of interest and convinced in his gut they were force-feeding him malarkey. In his senior year, he caught the mumps and never went back. He didn't know what to do with his windblown life. He went up to Kansas City and tried to enlist, but neither the Army nor the Navy wanted asthmatics with a reliance on the adrenalin needle. So he went off to the foundry . . . everybody in town went to the foundry sooner or later. The Sthals Foundry is in Kingsville, five miles west of Holden on 131, a dingy boxlike place filled with dust-smoke.

He ignored the smoke and was requisitioned his blowtorch. For eight hours each day, face-masked and wasting his breath, he worked at the far end of the gushing blue-white flame. He heard it whoosh and hiss for hours after he punched-out and drowned the noise in horse-gulps of iced beer at places like Hobb's Cafe on Nay Street in Holden—after he'd glutted himself with double burgers, korn dogs, and Susie-Qs at Herb's Drive-In on the Double-Y Highway in Peculiar.

There wasn't much to do when he got done with his blowtorch. He shot some pool at the Peculiar Recreation and Snack Bar, across the street from Herb's. It was here that he left one of the Peculiar merchants' kids bawling and pissing blood: Johnny

Sellers, a fancy-dancing high school halfback, blond burrheaded and handsome, just back from Marine Corps bootcamp, his nose in the high air.

It started at the Salt and Pepper Cafe, over too many beers, and somehow Charlie and Sellers both wound up at the Rec, shooting eightball at separate tables, until Sellers plunked his quarter down for the next game. Everybody knew there was going to be trouble, as if a funnel had been bleeped on the weatherman's radar screen. They came from opposite sides of the Missouri-Pacific tracks, the hayseed asthmatic and the merchant's leatherneck son, and stumbling into each other over cheeseburgers at a drive-in, there was an acrid tension between them, a smoldering of the wires, as each took disparaging high-headed glances at the other's machine. Sellers drove a spiffy fastback his father gave him for a birthday; Charlie drove whatever he could breathe life into at the yard.

Johnny Sellers plunked his quarter down and their first game ended fast. Two or three shots past the break, Johnny killed the eightball. The next game went the route, but ended with Charlie winning again, and the merchant's kid turned to the asthmatic and said: "Not too bad for somebody that can't fight!" There followed the ceremonial exchange of white-hot words: Sellers said something about the service and how asthma was a good excuse.

Charlie smashed a cuestick over the table and lashed at him, leaving a bloodied ridge at the side of his face. Sellers was bigger and he lunged, hooking a haymaker that missed. Charlie cracked him again with the stick, snapping it like a pencil over his chop-topped head, leaving Sellers dazed . . . then coldcocked him with both barrels as his knees flew high off the ground. Sellers crawled around on the floor; Charlie straightened him up and slammed his head against the pooltable. Blood rivered down the Marine's prettyboy showoff face.

The Marine's father made a complaint and the police questioned and wrote up a report. Not much was made of it; in towns like Holden and Peculiar, policemen like to stay out of redblooded matters, out of kidfeuds and wildoat scuffles settled near drive-ins or on the grimy floors of poolrooms.

Charlie stayed away from Peculiar for a while and spent much of his idling time by the Osage riverbank, fishing. He went with his rod and transistor radio, and brought home plastic bagfuls of largemouthed bass.

He was making pretty good money, a little better than $150 a week, and Bub worked at the foundry too, on the other side of the building. They were piling up a pisspot full of cash at the Holden Farmers and Commercial Bank and figured they might as well get some mileage out of it.

They decided to build a drag-racer. Not the banging/rattling kind they drove, but a highboy fastburning roadster which would be their dream car. A dream car cost a lot of money, sure, but they saw the day they'd get it all back . . . when, driven by Charlie or Bub Simpson, the dream car won record-time races at the strips in Kansas City and their picture appeared in blownup color on the cover of *Hot Rod* magazine.

They spent thousands of dollars. They bought torsion bars and rally wheels, constructed a superstock engine that would be a fireball howling down the track as the crowds—and the chicks wearing their "Keep on Trackin!" hotpants—cheered. They kept their dream car in the garage, suspended as if on an altar by barnyard blocks which were Charlie's invention. He took the beams from an abandoned barn, chainsawed them into twelve-inch slabs, then nailed drawer-handles on one end to make them easier to position.

The dream car was a chrome jezebel, sitting there on its altar blocks. Its hindtit flashed and sparkled like the shooting stars they'd skinned their eyes on when they were kids. Charlie was happy; he ogled his car for hours, mesmerized, absorbed in the gloss and the flash, seeing that pigrooting crowd knocked flat on its ass as Charlie Simpson—*winner*—blowtorched on by.

HE named the dream car Harry Scratch, which is what some folks call the devil. Right away it started behaving like it was witch-marked. Harry Scratch didn't win any races; it carried on like a black shecat had slinked under its hood and pissed there; it spun him around in slicks of bad luck and big bills.

They trucked it up to Kansas City the first time on a fossicating hot day when the sun was in the treetops. They had to pay money just to set it on the track. Seconds after Charlie got the flag and floored it, Harry Scratch belched-up a cloud of oily night-black smoke and sputtered to a stop. They took Harry back to Holden, doctored his crankshaft, paid out more money, and tried again. This time the manifold broke down. Then the connecting rod, the distributor, and the rocker arms, and each time it cost more and more and more money.

They were getting rawdealed, Charlie said to Bub. The parts they bought were booby-trapped and defective. None of these horrors had befallen them with the wrecked parts they resurrected from the junkyard. He got hold of a parts book with a price index. The money they'd been charged was at least $10 over bookprice. Index in hand, he drove to Kansas City to confront the cityslicker parts-man with his chicanery. What he had, the man told him, was a West Coast index. Cityslicker detailed shipping costs, itemized tax rates, and Charlie went back to Holden with the furious mute instinct they were getting screwed. He walked to the garage and kicked at Harry Scratch's body until his foot hurt, then hobbled back to Bub and said he was through with Harry Scratch and getting screwed.

"All they wanna do," he said, "is rob you."

He and Bub started drifting away from each other. Not because of Harry, but because of a squirmy girl Bub met; and when Bub told him he was getting married, Charlie nodded and allowed: "If you wanna go and get yourself pussywhipped, I'm not gonna stop you." Bub got married, moved into a new trailer, and just as Charlie suspected, started acting pussywhipped. He bought tons of appliances and worked sixteen hours a day in two foundries to foot the bills. He got off in Kingsville at 3:30, then nearly broke his fool neck to get to the other foundry, twenty-two miles away, by four o'clock. Charlie hooted and greened him as he got off at 3:30. "Poor old Bub, running like a bawlin'-hound with its tail 'tween his legs."

Harry Scratch, its fat shiny gut filled with money, was resting maddeningly in the garage, and Charlie, who'd go out now and occasionally to curse it, was having other problems. He spent his weekends hunting and fishing. He snared wiggling polebusters with his rod and tracked bucks with a borrowed Winchester 101, camping out for two or three days. Sometimes he missed the date with his blowtorch on Monday and blamed it on his asthma.

He didn't make many friends at the foundry. He stuck to himself and sunned outside while eating his peanut butter/jelly sandwich. When he let his hair creep down his back and stopped shaving, the men razzed him about being one of those creampuff hippie pantywaists. He took their joshing good-naturedly. The beard was furry armor against the blowtorch, he said. Maybe he'd get too close, they replied, and burn it off.

The foundry was cutting back; when he missed work on a Monday after one of his camping trips, he was fired. He went to his foreman and called him a "motherfucker." He claimed he had said he'd miss work that day and the man had agreed. The foreman denied it. Employees couldn't take vacations whenever they felt the mood and expect to get away with it.

"Fuck you!" Charlie said, and went home.

But he brooded. He thought it over and muttered to the old man about it. It wasn't right. He'd told the foreman he'd miss . . . They weren't going to get away with screwing him . . . If they wanted to let him go, since they were cutting back, that was allright . . . But they weren't going to lay any cock-and-bull into his file and call him a liar.

He went back to the foundry and stalked ramptiously into the personnel manager's office.

"Look, motherfucker!" he said, "I want this changed. I did notify you. I still wanna be fired, but I want it to read that I notified you and you let me go."

Bejesus scared out of him by this demon-eyed raving hippie, the personnel manager complied. The next week Charlie filed for unemployment.

He talked about Harry Scratch out there on its blocks. Harry was still a good way to make money; he'd sell the bastard piece by piece and drink beer off his parts for a while. But Bub, good old housebroken Bub, fixed that. Bub said his new wife wanted him to get rid of the car. Right away. Fast. For cash.

They were business partners, so Charlie stood by as Bub zipped around the countryside and sold Harry Scratch for garage sale prices. When the last part was gone, Charlie figured Harry had cost them $9,000. He told his little brother he was like the rest of them—out to guzzle money. He piled the barnyard blocks high in a corner. It was all that was left of his vainglorious dreams: a leaning-post for his fishing pole and the old man's coyote gun.

OUT of work, with Harry Scratch bartered into thin air, he floundered in apathy and boredom. Outside Chilhowee, on Route 2, behind a hiding-wall of towering oak, past the sign that hustles "Nixon Feeds," he stumbled onto the ruins of an ancient boxcar. Its roof had collapsed, its sides were corrugated and infirm. He squatted there. He gunned his new/old Chevy behind the oak and spent his days in the ruins . . . with bottles of hogkilling redwine, gun and tackle magazines, kinky mailordered Japanese fuckbooks, and each day's edition of the *Kansas City Star.*

When the wind turned icy and rain slushed his boxcar, he built a charcoal campfire. He refused to be driven out, but he caught fever and wound up in bed for a week. The squatter stopped going back to his ruins after that.

He drove the backroads, going nowhere in particular. He whipped his Chevy around S-curves away from the mainroads and highways. He knew the cops would nail him and it would cost more money. Driving down Bypass 71 outside Harrisonville, he turned onto a country lane. Surrounded by a weedchoked lawn and sagging wire fence, he saw a little house with the letters E-G-A-D on its shingled roof. On the side of its brickwall was a hand-painted jumbo-sized American flag. Clusters of longhairs gulled around on the lawn. He anchored his Chevy and walked over, a gaunt rawboned figure with tarpaper black hair, and found a home.

EGAD was a coffeehouse, built for the kids of Harrisonville by a middle-aged Jesus Freak. Its letters meant "Everybody Give A Damn!"

It gave a damn, first, about Future Farmers of America-type projects, staging a halftime variety show for a Wildcat football game, but as it attracted more kids, the talk swirled around the War, racism, rock, and dope. There were but three rules: No booze! No dope! No hassling! Charlie realized fast only the third rule was observed. EGAD's doors were never closed; the loosest times, therefore, were at three and four o'clock in the morning, when he and a half dozen others, Win Allen among them, mounted a candle on the floor, smoked a few joints, and passed the wine. He didn't feel down-to-his toes loose there yet—he called Win Allen "rughead" and "nigger"—but he was attracted by the instant blind fellowship, the warmth, and the music.

Some of the kids at EGAD wore Mod Squad clothes, knits and landlubbers, skinny-ribs and tie-dyed Levis, while he wore his baggy farmers' denims, butternut overalls, and hand-me-down shirts. He took $200 out of the bank and went on a buying spree in Kansas City. He had his hair styled and razorcut and picked up loud bellbottoms and splashy flowered shirts. When he went back to EGAD, he was pimped about becoming a "city sissy," and he replied, looking straight-on at Win: "I got tired of looking like a fucking field nigger."

Shortly after dawn one day, Charlie and Win and a few others drove a Volkswagen camper to a wheatfield in western Cass County. Armed with butcher knives and sickles, they attacked the beanstalk-high marijuana plants flowering there. They were happy about their commando raid, stuffed the camper heaping with grass, and drove the haul to a shed near the boxcar. He was smoking more dope (the fields were an eden of grass), becoming first sullenly aloof and then schoolgirl giggly when he smoked.

But too many townies were giving a God-fearing damn about EGAD by then, getting high on stories of marijuana-induced orgies. ("It can turn you into a degenerate," Sheriff Bill Gough said.) The civic yelping got so loud Police Chief Bill Davis's men couldn't ignore it anymore. First they'd turned it a deaf ear . . . EGAD, truth be told, wasn't in the town proper. Hell, it was miles from the courthouse and the square . . . but now tobacco-chewing narks lurked in the trees jotting license numbers down. Housing inspectors visited every day. After five or six citations, the housing office closed EGAD for a faulty electrical socket— a "fire hazard." The house with the American flag on its side was boarded up and padlocked.

It was warming then, though. The ice-storms were passing, the shitepokes and dunkadoos were back in their nests, and Charlie took some of his friends to the boxcar. They piled their ruins high with feedbags full of grass, and used the fishnets which once hung on the EGAD's walls for interior decoration.

They met two mustached servicemen from Richardson-Gebaur Airbase (halfway up the Interstate to Kansas City), and took the soldiers to their boxcar. They gave them Bud and grass. One of the airmen, who'd been stationed in Germany, said their weed was good enough to sell. The airmen wanted to make a deal: to buy kilos of the stuff and then resell it for tidy profit in Kansas City. But the muscles in Charlie's cheeks flexed hard and he said no.

"We're not going to sell it for any money," he said. "If somebody wants to come down for it, we'll give it to 'em." He was angry. He told the airmen they were money-grubbers, just like everybody else, but he could dig it because "Sam pounds that shit into everybody."

They were sitting around one day, talking about money and clothes, and Charlie said the biggest money-grubbers always wore the nicest threads. So he brought his spiffy new flowered shirts and landlubbers to the boxcar and gave them away. Except for his favorite silver-zippered tanktop, which was thrown on the charcoal in his ruins, and sacramentally burned.

"I blow a fart," he told the old man, "and sirens go off." It was getting bad: cops got together over slices of free apple pie at Herb's Drive-In and were overheard joking about the times they'd "shot down" Charlie Simpson's jalopy. Applesauce Wakeman clipped him two days straight on a dirtroad off Route 2, which meant they'd wised-up to his cowpath-traveling habits and were trapping for him in the boonies.

On a cold spring day, the old man asked him to pick up some chairs in Lone Jack. Charlie didn't want to go, but the old man insisted and he said allright, what the hell. He didn't want to drive his Chevy because the cops would buzz down on him. He borrowed a neighbor's pickup. He drove in pitchforking rain and heard the siren serenading him as he got into Lone Jack. He knew he hadn't been speeding.

"What the hell's wrong?" he said.

It was a routine vehicle inspection, the highway patrolman said, and led him to a patrol way-station outside of town.

The patrolman checked his identification and his Selective Service card. He ran steel-eyes over his bluejeans and Army fatigue jacket, and said: "Your hair's sure nice and long, boy, aint it?"

He climbed into the pickup, checked the idiot lights, brakes, headlights, and steering. Then he tugged on the emergency brake and said it was defective. Charlie got in, gave it a yank, and said it worked fine.

"You got twenty-five minutes to fix it," the cop said, "or you're under arrest."

"It's raining."

"That long hair's gonna get wet," the patrolman said.

"I ain't got the tools."

The patrolman said that was his tough luck.

Charlie said the patrolman could go get fucked.

He was arrested and faced two charges: operating an unsafe motor vehicle and abusing a police officer.

He told his friends he'd been messed-over because of his scarecrow freak hair and swore they'd never make him cut it. "I'm gonna grow it till I can wrap my prick in it," he said.

"One of these days," he told Win. "I'm not gonna let these pigs push me around and then they're gonna learn to leave me alone."

A month after he paid $50 for the pleasure of telling the highway patrolman to get fucked, he was riding with Duane Bailey, a bushy-bearded buddy from Peculiar. They were a mile outside Kingsville, in Duane's faultless '66 Ford, when they were stopped. They were taken out of the car, spreadeagled, frisked, and escorted to the cruiser. Duane was cited for driving a car with a faulty exhaust.

"You can't give me a ticket," Duane said, "we're outside of town."

"The sheriff can give you a ticket," the cop laughed, and requested assistance from the Cass County sheriff's office.

If he wasn't under arrest, Duane said, he didn't have to wait for the sheriff to get there. The cop "advised" him to wait.

"I'm not getting any ticket," Charlie said, "I don't have to wait."

He took Duane's keys, leaped behind the Ford's wheel, and punched it into a careening U-turn right in front of the cops. He stuck his arm out the window, honked the horn, and gave the cops his rigid middle finger.

He raced the car to Holden, left its motor running, and slammed through the front door.

"Where in hell's the fire?" the old man asked.

"Got a date with the can," he said.

He grabbed Bub's motorcycle helmet, goggles and gloves, and headed the Ford back toward Kingsville.

A roadblock waited for him two miles from the spot he'd left Duane. Doing more than 100 m.p.h., he skirted two sheriff's cars, leapfrogged a field, knocked down a fence, and was back on the highway with the sheriff's cars in fire-breathing pursuit.

Duane was still sitting in the back of the Kingsville cruiser, which Charlie almost rammed as he braked the Ford to a shrieking blood-curdling stop less than a hairbreadth behind it.

A cop got out of the cruiser, whey-faced and horror-struck, his gun drawn, and pointed it at him. The cop's finger was on the trigger and the finger trembled.

Charlie got out of the Ford . . . The Bingbuffer himself in helmet, goggles, and gloves . . . lifted a hand within inches of the cop's pale face, waved it limp-wristed, and said: "Howdy do, partner!" . . . whinnying like a puddinhead all the way to jail.

HE was lured to the square by dirty old men who recalled a bygone America patinaed with gunsmoke and romance. The Cass County Retirement Home is kittycorner to the courthouse, and these grizzled graybeards, wrapped in motheaten raincoats, birchwood canes in their hands, tapped to the Harrisonville Hotel lobby each morning, where they smoked noxious Marsh-Wheeling stogies, and then crossed the street to the courthouse. Some of them shuffled to the basement, where a boiler room was their casino, and played penny-a-hand poker. Others were content to sit on the steps and the wooden bench left there for their arthritis—content to stretch in the shade listening to leaves' whispers and pickup trucks' backfires.

Charlie came to hear them historify, with florid doddering eloquence, about things they'd heard tell or seen with their own rheumy eyes . . . horses and buggies that once lined the square . . . the Wells-Fargo stagecoach that stopped at the Allen Bank once a week . . . the nigger that got burned alive over Marysville way after he defiled a schoolmarm in her own classroom. Win and Rise Risner, Jimson Thompson, Gary Hale and George Russell, came around and greased their memories with Thunderbird and Cribari. When their tales got dull and self-winding, the old winebibbers lost their hoary charm.

But Charlie and his friends stayed on the square, set up camp yards from these toothless specters, because they saw now, in each vile passing townie glance, the validity of their trip, the justification of their self-imposed isolation. They wallowed in it, exaggerating everything . . . their saintliness and martyrdom . . . their refusal to play the game by the lowly rules of their parents . . . and created a sideshow.

They were hometown hippies who primped in the cracked mirror of their egos and saw themselves as more intelligent, more humane, more real than their plastic deodorized elders. They were the victims of a freeze-dried generational racism which would not forgive their long loathsome hair and their scuzzy tramp-clothes. So now, cast in a psychodrama partly of their own design, they grew their hair even longer and let their jeans get grubbier. They asked for it: the audience reaction was confirmation of all their halfbaked theories. They screamed "Fuck You!" with every gesture and found applause in cops' teeth-gnashings and housewives' cringings.

Charlie was shaping a crude and jumbled socio-political philosophy, helped by Win, Rise, Jimson Thompson and their readings of Rubin and Hoffman. He viewed himself as an innocent persecuted by "pigs" and lipsynched those bloodshot burlesque phrases: "Off the pig!" and "Up against the wall, motherfucker!" He was taking Rubin and Hoffman literally, as seriously as he had once taken *being* Cole Younger, not comprehending that much of his generation had by then dismissed Jerry and Abbie as clowns . . . countercultural gagsters . . . who deadpanned naive believers into jails and Inner Turmoil . . . while they romped on the NBC Nightly News.

Jerry and Abbie's style directed their sideshow, with Charlie one of its surefire stars. The star sat on the courthouse steps and lewd-eyed farmers' wives as they ankled their porkfed asses by and said things to them like: "Hey, you want some, mam?" . . . Or, after straightening his arm, then bending it up at the elbow, he inquired: "Excuse me, mam, how much of this you want?" He was known, too, for his whoop. Once or twice an afternoon, as the merchants ministered to their money, their bookkeeping was rent by a scream . . . "Eeeeee! Yaaaaa! Eeeeee! Yaaaaa! Yaaaaa! Yaaaaa!" . . . that made white-haired Lloyd Foster in his drugstore feel like he was in the middle of a loonyhouse.

Their sideshow featured an outrageous psychosexual twist which called on the rughead, Win Allen, and the town's Southern tradition. They discovered, occupying the square, that they had bewitched a children's army of impressionable disciples: high school kids in adolescent revolt against the authority of their parents. They flocked to the square, these fifteen- sixteen- seventeen-year-olds, many of them girls, not just because the hippies were there (associating with hippies was a guaranteed way to raise their parents' blood-pressure) but because Win Allen was there . . . the Nigger was there!

So the pubescent daughters of these oldline Dixie patriots wiggled up to the square, and in full elevated view of the entire town, put their arms around the Nigger! and kissed his ithyphallic jigaboo ass! and played the parts of people their parents hated worse even than niggers. They became monkey-fuckers and coons' whores; delicate white flowers fondling black jawbreaker cock. And Win Allen, being no fool and being young and proud, discovered he could niggerlip and blackguard white titties in sunny white-racist daylight—right in the middle of town!

Charlie and Win played another game which made the same point. One of their Bros drove a black-curtained Volkswagen camper to the courthouse. Win went inside with a dimpled high school girl while Charlie proclaimed, in offkey auctioneer voice, "Yeah, Win's in there fucking a skunk again." Sure enough, the palefaced townspeople could see the camper gently rocking in shameless licentious rhythm. Most times, Win wasn't fucking

. . . only diabolically mindfucking Harrisonville. He went into the camper with his high school girl, arm in arm, and they hopped up and down on the mattress in the back, fully clothed and cackling, making sure it looked wicked and promiscuous from the outside. Because while a lot of these pink-cheeked little girls didn't want to fuck Win Allen, they wanted it to *look* like they were fucking him.

One night, stoned on wine and grass, seven or eight of them sat in a circle on the courthouse lawn, and Charlie, increasingly vain about the benefits of his "cocksicle," zipped his pants down. A seventeen-year-old dropout, a Drive-In hotsy the grapevine rated one of the "town pigs," went down on him openmouthed and gave him hogwild head, which the others observed and applauded.

They were careful, these sideshow freaks, to plant telltale self-incriminating evidence on the courthouse lawn: wine-bottles, prophylactics, a ketchup-smeared pair of nylon panties. They knew the groundskeeper had orders to collect the evidence and hand-deliver it to the Cass County Juvenile Officer, Everett Wade, whose office was two floors up in the courthouse, directly overlooking what he called "Sodom and Gonorrhea."

"**IF** the Lord wanted men to be dogs," his father told him, hearing about the blowjob on the square, "He'd made them dogs." Charlie didn't take to the old man's sermonizing. "The Revolution's gonna come!" he told him, "everybody's gonna live like dogs!"

High on rhetoric, he said that when the Revolution came, the pigs hassling him would be the first to pay. The sins of Applesauce Wakeman would be avenged.

He sat on the square in screwball communion with his Bros and they reassured each other the impending Revolution would deliver them from evil. That after the shitstorm, pig redneck blood would be hosed to the gutters and they'd build their human loving peaceful world in the stench-filled streets. (Never mind the obvious grotesqueries, even their timing was absurd: they promised themselves the Revolution in the autumn of 1971, a time when the anti-war movement was withering and campus concerns once again were finals, jobs, and menstrual cycles.)

But they lived in a cave. The square isolated them not only from common horse-sense, but from their less countrified generational peers, and reading Rubin and Hoffman the way their parents read the King James Bible, they waited for the grass to be burned and the downpour of hail and fire mingled with blood. They were zealots of the Cause, wildfiring the Word, ready, when the time came, to Do It! to off the pigs! for the Revolution!

"It's the only way," Charlie said, "fight fire with fire, kill or be killed."

"How can you off the pigs and love your brothers at the same time?" George Russell asked.

And Charlie immediately changed his mind: "Yeah, I guess that's right."

Awaiting cleansing devastation, they avoided ideological quarrels among themselves. They were brothers, all of them wearing the same make-up to play the same roles, speaking the same hip-farcical language. So they left tactical decisions—like murder —to the future and proselytized melodramatically. They glared at the merchants on the square and said the Revolution was coming, implying that on that earthshaking day their storewindows best not be chalked with peace symbols of doom. The money-grubbers could avoid holocaust by not hassling them—or else!

One afternoon something crunched against Lloyd Foster's drugstore window. When he looked out, he saw a few diehard Retirement Home crocks tottering from the courthouse as fast as their canes could take them. The hippies were scampering like ratbit-fevered maniacs across the street. They were armed with what looked like grenades, which they lobbed at each other and at passing cars. Lord God! Lloyd Foster thought, the Revolution he'd heard about had finally come! He called the sheriff and locked and bolted the door.

On the courthouse lawn, Charlie Simpson was chasing a high school kid. When he was only a few feet from him, Charlie wound up and fired. He hit the kid in the back. The kid staggered, lurched, and fell on his face. Charlie stepped over the kid's body and saw Win crouched behind the Marine Corps recruitment sign. He took off after him. His pockets bulged with more ammo. He fired them as Win dodged across Independence Street and headed for the water tower behind the Retirement Home. Cars

were honking and some of the drivers were shaking their fists
... the hippies were going batshit in some ague-fit ... storeowners
looked up from crossword puzzles and saw longhairs hurling
themselves between cars with demented kamikaze gleams in their
eyes.

The sheriff's deputies got to the courthouse just as Rise
Risner caught one in the temple. He was blown to the stone by
the impact and flopped there like they do in John Wayne movies.
A deputy ran to him and Risner cocked one eye open and said:
"Sshh, I'm dead." They raised him up. They were giving him the
business when Win came flying toward them, Charlie still behind
him, firing and missing with each shot as Win high-stepped like
a ballet-dancer. "Allright, goddamnit," the deputy hollered,
"you're all under arrest!"

They told the dumbfounded deputy they were having a war
—"nothing to get riled about, man," said Win—between the
Pigs and the Bros. They'd flipped coins: the losers were Pigs, the
winners were Bros, and they were fighting to the death. Win
laughed. "I'm a pig," he said, "Ootney's a bro."

It was a *game*, Win said. They'd driven the camper out No.
7 Highway to a row of evergreen trees and rooted around in the
pinestraw picking up pine-cones. They counted them up and
divided them equally between Pigs and Bros. Then, at exactly
three o'clock, Charlie Simpson blew a Boy Scout whistle. They
had ten minutes to entrench themselves, after which the whistle
blew again and fighting began. That's all there was to it, Win said,
they were *playing*.

Now, Win said, he had Pigs scattered all over town. The war
wasn't over yet, and like a good warzone commander, he had to
count his bodies and his kills.

"That's right, pig," Charlie said.

"You calling me a pig?" the deputy asked.

"Naw," Charlie said, "Win's the pig."

It was altogether too much to handle for two sheriff's deputies whose only police training had been the Report-Making Class in Kansas City and who'd been summoned to the scene of the Revolution . . . only to find the hippies killing each other in madcap fun with an arsenal of pine-cones.

Nothing could be done, anyway. There was no statute against having a pine-cone war on the square. The deputies went back to the sheriff's office; Win went off to body-count dead pigs; Charlie loaded up with more ammo.

The Bros won. The pigs paid the price. Led by Win Allen, they snorted around the courthouse toting shopping bags, collecting spent pine-cones, as Charlie Simpson, revolutionary Bro hero, yelled: "Pick 'em up, nigger! Get your black ass in gear!"

WAITING for apocalypse, a pine-cone warrior playing empty-headed kidgames, he stumbled along by guess and by God. Even his opinions windmilled chaotically. Sometimes, Rise recalls, he took both sides of the same issue, turning his back on contradictions. He argued for blood and violence and moments later exploded: "I never said any of that shit. I don't believe like that." To flip-flop all over the place and deny everything got to be known as one of Ootney's Acts.

They called him Ootney because of a shriveled geezer named Jimbob Jones who ran a carryout on No. 7 Highway a few miles from town. Jimbob took a shine to Charlie Simpson and whenever he sauntered in with his Bros for quarts of strawberry wine and sixpacks of Bud, Jimbob rollicked: "Well, looky here, rootin' tootin' Mr. Simpson." So Win and Rise called him Rootin' Tootin' at first, then Tootney and gradually bastardized it into Ootney.

Ootney told them one day about this cat he came upon. He'd been down at the Cass County Library, reading . . . Win danced a jig he thought that was so funny . . . about this cat Henry David Thoreau, which he pronounced Toe-Row. He read about his life and read some of his writings and this cat really had his shit together . . . Toe-Row knew better than anybody that Life is a Big Fat Asshole with everybody trying to Stick It To You when they get half the chance. They listened to him, laughed, and winked at what they figured was another of Ootney's half-cocked Acts. Which was confirmed when Ootney said old Toe-Row had it more together than anybody he could think of outside of George C. Wallace, and Win rejoiced until he got the hiccups.

"Oww, man! George C. Wallace?"

"He's full of a lot of horseshit," Ootney said, "yeah. But he doesn't fuck around. He don't lie like the others. He tells you what he feels."

He kept preaching Henry David Toe-Row as the weeks went by, finally got into a hassle with Win over Whose Shit Was More Together? Toe-Row's? or Abbie Hoffman's?

To win his point, he gave them a hand-tailored adaptation of Toe-Row's life . . . Old Toe-Row was a far-out lonesome dude who built a school with his brother, then got tight with another weird cat, Ralph Waldo Emerson, and they formed this group . . . like the group they had here on the square . . . only they weren't called hippies then, they were called Trans-Sin-Dentalists. Toe-Row and Ralph Waldo believed religion had shit nor shinola to do with churches, that everybody is born with beamrays which detect vibes and tell what's bogosity from what's genuine. Old Henry David even worked in Ralph Waldo's house as a servant or handyman, something lowrate, because he didn't believe it's important what you do as long as you dig living.

. . . Then Henry David built a hut down by a pond and he lived there for years, grooving on his own head, the earth, the weather . . . Wasn't chickenshit, either . . . The cat had horse's balls . . . Figured out the government was screwing him just like everybody else and went to jail instead of paying his taxes.

Ootney said he was going to live just like Toe-Row: find a plot of land somewhere, build one of those rockhouses the Osage Indians used to have, take his fishing pole out there, get high sitting around like a barefoot redskin king.

One day he waved a sheet of loose-leaf paper which was filled on both sides with his pained bigletter scrawling. He wanted to read this outloud because these were the things Toe-Row and the Trans-Sin-Dentalists believed in. When he finished reading it, he tucked the paper into a dog-eared copy of *Walden,* where it was found less than a year later . . . *tagged as evidence: (State of Missouri Highway Patrol Supplementary Investigation Report, page six. Subject: Charles Simpson, deceased. Nature of crime: homicide.)*

The piece of paper was in a bulging rubber-banded file, at the bottom of which were six technicolored Polaroid glossies: Ootney, his eyes wide, raw naked, grapefruit-sized brown-red crater in the top of his head.

The piece of paper said:

THOREAU

I THINK THAT WE SHOULD BE MEN FIRST AND SUBJECTS AFTER-WARD. IT IS NOT DESIRABLE TO CULTIVATE A RESPECT FOR THE LAW AS MUCH AS FOR THE RIGHT.

I WAS DETERMINED TO KNOW BEANS.

THE SAVAGE IN MAN IS NEVER QUITE ERADICATED.

BEWARE OF ALL ENTERPRISES THAT REQUIRE NEW CLOTHES.

IT IS LIFE NEAR THE BONE WHERE IT IS SWEETEST.

LOVE YOUR LIFE, POOR AS IT IS.

IT IS CHARACTERISTIC OF WISDOM NOT TO DO DESPERATE THINGS.

MEN ARE WHAT THEY ARE, BUYING AND SELLING AND SPENDING THEIR LIVES LIKE SERFS.

HOW DOES IT BECOME A MAN TO BEHAVE TOWARD THIS AMERICAN GOVERNMENT TODAY? I ANSWERED THAT HE CANNOT WITHOUT DISGRACE BE ASSOCIATED WITH IT.

FIRE IS THE MOST TOLERABLE THIRD PARTY.

I SAW THAT THE STATE WAS HALFWITTED AND THAT IT DID NOT KNOW ITS FRIENDS FROM ITS FOES. I LOST ALL MY REMAINING RESPECT FOR IT AND PITIED IT.

THE MASS OF MEN LEAD LIVES OF QUIET DESPERATION.

I AM A MASS OF VAIN STRIVINGS TIED BY A CHANCE BOND TOGETHER.

IN THE LONG RUN MEN HIT ONLY WHAT THEY AIM AT.

DIG IT!

FUCKING was the only thing Toe-Row got all wrong. "A woman would be a foe to my career," the Trans-Sin-Dentalist wrote, and Ootney told Rise: "Old Henry David, he must not have liked to fuck."

Ootney loved to fuck. He could fuck all night, Rise recalls, and ask for more. He was their stud, a peckerwood satyr who bragged about getting up in the morning, beating off . . . going down to the square, getting laid . . . seeing a movie at the Drive-In, getting head . . . going home, beating off again.

Sex was no problem: they attracted girls to the square the way the land attracted the wind. If the girl wanted to stay with them for their whole trip, if she wasn't just passing through like one of those knock-kneed wallflower types—then she had to behave like a trueblue revolutionary sister . . . and spread her farmgirl thighs whenever and wherever they wanted. It was a test of the sisters' dedication. Their Bro Revolution had nothing to do with Women's Lib and sexual equality. Girls lucky enough to be their skunk/sisters were sweating pieces of ass sometimes passed like lapdogs around a campfire . . . shuttlecocked back and forth by these doltish high-minded innocents who joystuck hungry cocksicles into them . . . sisters sometimes called skunk/bitch/cunt but never Ms. There were four or five of these sisters' cycle gangs call mamas, and Ootney, who first used the word "cocksicle" with the pride some folks save for their bragdog, took his turn with them all.

The cocksicle seemed his only link to the opposite sex, though there was a girl in a town near Holden, a drive-in carhop he met over a korn dog. He saw her now and then, but never with his Bros. She is a simple working girl who wants to make good; she waitresses at truckstops and burgerstands and dreams about being a secretary in a carpeted Harrisonville office. She has short rust-colored hair often up in curlers, a pale pimpled complexion, and a body which is the victim of too may Cokes and greasy french fries. She was as afraid of the hippies on the square as Lloyd Foster or G.M. Allen, and whenever Charlie drove her home and stayed in her immaculate two-room apartment, she begged him to go back to the foundry and apologize . . . to get a job at the Chevy plant in Raytown . . . to get away from those shiftless branchwater longhairs. He never argued, said only: "Aww, they're allright." He never bragged about his cocksicle, either, never mentioned the Revolution, and they never fucked or P-ed down: they made love. Which ended when she got a rash and then a suspicious discharge and stopped seeing him but didn't see a doctor either, because she was afraid he'd tell her she had gonorrhea.

He enjoyed playing the backwoods Tarzan with the horsecock of steel, and never said anything to his Bros about the semitender visits to his pimpled carhop. He told Rise: "Love is just a crock of shit, look at Bub. Bub gets married and he says it's true love. He kills himself to buy her a mountain of shit and he piles up fucking bills. Now he says he shouldn't have got married and it isn't true love. He's getting a divorce and he's still got to pay the bills. Now he's gonna have laywer bills and then he's gonna have alimony bills."

He announced, too, that he'd stopped using prophylactics because they were "unnatural." If men were meant to wear rubbers, they'd have been born with a flop of skin which could be worn the way hats are worn against the cold. He'd take his chances. If he got a dose and came bad, he'd learn something by the disease. If he got a sister/skunk pregnant, she'd have the baby and he'd take care of it when he got his rockhouse by the pond.

He and one of his Bros drove to Kansas City one night, white-hunting black whores, because Ootney'd heard there was nobody as smooth on a cocksicle as a black whore with pearly white teeth. The two farmboys didn't know what they were do-ing. They drove around the ghetto alleys they were told to seek, until a flashy spade wearing a gold-gleaming gambler's hat crooked a finger at them. They stopped the car and the spade said he could provide the party they were looking for.

Cocksure, they made the deal. It would cost them $30 a/-piece to head around the world. They could hand over half the money now and the gold-gleaming spade would give them the address. They went for it, these revolutionary soozy heroes, handed their cash over, wrote the address down, and walked up three flights of tenement stairs to an apartment. A bald pot-bellied black man answered and said: "What you want?"

Ootney checked the address and told the man it was allright: they'd been directed there and they paid their money, the man didn't have to play games . . . The black man with the potbelly ranted and raved. This was the one-thousandth time snotnosed whiteboys had barged up in the middle of the night looking for a party . . . unless they got the sweetfuck out of there, he'd call the cops. Murphied like two rube teenagers looking for their first piece, the revolutionaries left the ghetto and went back to their square.

Rise, blessed with a coarse sense of humor, savored his friend's sexual exploits, and remembers watching Ootney in action on a sunkissed spring day out in the woods. Barechested, his arms around the trunk of a big-assed oak, holding onto it so his biceps popped out, dingus pressed up against the bark, hips bumping and grinding. Ootney the Trans-Sin-Dentalist was fucking the tree.

IN 1839 Henry David Thoreau, accompanied by his brother, spent a week sailing the Concord and Merrimack rivers. In the late fall of 1971 Charlie Simpson, squirrel-shooting nature-lover, thought he'd ape old Henry David's example. He'd spend a week, accompanied by one of his Bros, sailing the Mississippi River. He was reminded that some Teeny-Bros named Huck Finn and Tom Sawyer had already done that, so he went to see them.

Huck Finn and Tom Sawyer stand in a tourist-trap square of their own in Hannibal, Missouri, a four-hour drive from Harrisonville, and a town which still makes money off the ghost of Mark Twain. Huck Finn and Tom Sawyer have been transmogrified into stone, targets of pigeonshit and tot-wonder, hustlers of vacationers' dollars. Ootney drove to Hannibal to scout the river and to dig on Huck Finn.

Huck Finn is protected from madmen and vandals by a knee-high fence with tulips growing behind it. When Ootney paid his admission and stood eyeball-to-eyeball with Huck, he thought the fence was a silly hindrance. He stepped over it, and at a time of year when few others were there, sat at the base of the statue . . . the better to dig Huck's vibes.

The cops came, summoned by a ticket-taker who looked up disbelievingly to see a hippie with black pirate hair acting like he was doped at Huck Finn's feet.

"What you doing there, boy?" the cop asked.

"Sitting here," he said.

Normal folks didn't sit around Huck Finn's feet, so the cops took him to their cruiser, patted him down, made him empty his pockets, spilled his cigarettes out of their pack, checked his identification, hoped for a warrant in the centrex, and were forced to let him go . . . almost.

"How'd you get here, boy?"

When he told them about his car in the lot, facing Huck's back, they wanted to see it. When they saw it, they wanted to see every inch of it. They emptied his ashtray, sniffed the butts, ransacked the glove compartment, stuck their hands under the seats, and found nothing. It was time then for the Routine Vehicle Inspection, and sure as shit his ass was in a sling. The turn signal didn't work and he was cited (the cops snickering as they wrote out the ticket) while Huck Finn, a money-grubber like the rest of them, looked the other way. He went back to the square and told them: sitting by statues was a crime, Huck Finn was bad karma, the river was sewer-dirty and bummed him out. His Toe-Row trip was off.

A month later, he was jabbering about going to Kansas City to see a rock concert. Black Sabbath, his favorite group, was coming to town. Black Sabbath plays garbage rock, their decibel level is their music: exactly the kind of shrill anti-melodic sound he loved. He dug Black Sabbath, too, because he thought they were evil . . . (they pretend a choreographed chthonic fury; their guitars ooze noise some confuse with aconite and henbane).

He drove to Kansas City a week before the concert and paid $7 for a frontrow ticket. He drove to the city early the day of the show, hoping to find out where Black Sabbath was staying. When he got there, he discovered he'd lost his ticket.

He panicked, afraid the show would be sold out, and went to the concert boxoffice. It was closed.

He drove to a department store where they were selling tickets. They were sold out.

He drove to another. They were sold out, too.

Halfway back to Harrisonville, in Grandview, he was told, a record store still had some tickets. He got back on the Interstate, drove to Grandview, and bought another $7 frontrow ticket.

Two hours before the concert, he was walking around downtown Kansas City when, in front of the public library, he ran into Duane Bailey, the buddy from Peculiar who'd been with him the night he dressed up like the Bingbuffer and almost got shot by the cops.

He told Duane he was going to see Black Sabbath and asked if he wanted to go. Duane wanted to go, but didn't have a ticket. Ootney said they were still selling tickets at the record store in Grandview.

Duane didn't have any money, either. Ootney gave him the money.

Duane didn't have a ride—to get back to Grandview to buy the ticket with Ootney's money. Ootney offered him the ride.

They got back on the Interstate again, fighting rush-hour traffic, back to Grandview for the second time, this time for Duane's ticket. The record store was closed.

Maybe the boxoffice, Ootney said, had tickets after all. They raced back to Kansas City but were twenty minutes late. There were plenty of tickets left. They had to pay full price, even though the concert had begun. Since he had a $7 frontrow seat, he bought Duane a $7 frontrow seat.

They hustled to their seats. The seats were filled: ripped-off and liberated by brother longhairs who bought cheap seats and stole the good ones. What could they do? Even the aisles were jammed with kids.

Ootney the revolutionary appealed to the ushers. The ushers

shrugged their shoulders. They weren't about to go wading into a longhaired mob just so two other longhairs could get their right seats.

He and Duane sat near the backrow, $7 frontrow tickets in their hands. The acoustics were crummy: Black Sabbath sounded like a freight train roaring by with its whistle broken but tooting.

When they got outside, he offered Duane a ride back to Peculiar. He had to take a piss first, and didn't feel like fighting the crowd back inside to the john. He went down an alley behind the stagedoor and let her rip against the side of the hall.

His cocksicle got caught in the zipper . . . the squad car came tooling down the alley, its outraged cherry blazing. He was arrested for indecent exposure and spent the night in jail.

Next morning the piss cost him $100.

STREET-PEOPLE at the University of
Kansas, he heard, were liberating Lawrence, a three-hour drive
from Harrisonville. He went there two weekends and disliked
almost everything about the place. Cops stalked the bars with
Japanese billyclubs, Mace, and babyblue helmets. Paranoia was a
contagious disease: undercover narks and FBI men shadowed the
rooftops with infrared Snooperscopes. Most of the longhairs
weren't street-people at all, but "Plastic Hippies," children of
bogosity and split-level suburbia who spoke counterfeit hip and
studied computerized ways to make money.

Their scene in Harrisonville, he told Rise and Win, was more
real than the plastic hippies' flimflamming. The longhairs at U.K.
didn't give a shit about the Revolution and the war. They were
copouts who'd given up the fight . . . pigs camouflaged with long
hair who'd see the barber the day before they went jobhunting
. . . their war against war canceled because their cockered patch-
oulied skins were safe from the draft.

The only thing he liked about Lawrence was the Angel. The
Angel is a twenty-nine-year-old drifter, a professional nonstudent
who thumbs from campus to campus. A campus always has part-
time jobs, he says, and full-time chicks free with their body fluids
and Daddy's money. No one seems to know his full name; everyone calls him the Angel. He looks like a longhaired sumo wrestler,
a hitman on some nazified communal karma squad. He stands an

easy 6 foot 3, weighs 275 pounds. He wears his hair in a ponytail and sometimes a patch over the left eye. There is nothing wrong with his left eye. He is called the Angel because he claims he was once a member of the Oakland chapter of the Hell's Angel, sitting at the right hand of Sonny Barger himself.

Besides being a professional leech, the Angel is a pathological liar. He produces elaborate pulp-fiction fables in which he casts himself as a swashbuckling countercultural soldier of fortune. He left the Angels because they were sissified into movie stars. He dated one of the two girls killed at Kent State: "Sarah Schwartz." He and Mick Jagger got to be tight during the Stones' tour. Blah blah blah.

Charlie Simpson met the Angel in a bar on the Strip in Lawrence, and the Angel told him about his adventures with the Weatherman, whom he joined after ignoring Sonny Barger's pleas to stay. When the Angel told him about his old childhood pal Abbie Hoffman, Charlie invited him to meet his Bros on the square.

The revolutionary who once pretended he was Cole Younger and the visionary Hell's Angel once bosom-buddy to Abbie Hoffman seemed made for each other. Charlie chauffeured him to Harrisonville one weekend, where the Angel smoked a lot of their dope, fucked one of their skunks, drank sixpacks of beer, and nonchalantly reminisced about the times he and Abbie played stickball. Abbie was cool even then, even when the Angel beat him all the time. The Angel agreed with Charlie that most of the people in Lawrence were pussies and vehemently right-on-ed their cornpone Revolution.

Charlie was proud of his worldwise new friend. The Angel had seen it all, been everywhere, done everything, knew how to live. The Angel was a Bro they could rely on. Maybe he could talk him into coming down to Harrisonville, living there, helping them turn-on the town. Maybe the two of them could get an apartment and smoke dope, fuck, and drink beer. Maybe when he got his land, he'd ask the Angel to move in with him (just like old Toe-Row and Ralph Waldo Emerson) and they'd groove on being Bros with each other and the world around them.

When Charlie read about an anti-war march in Washington, D.C., he asked the Angel to go with him. He'd never been to an anti-war march, and since the Angel was a friend of Abbie's they might be able to see Abbie and spend some time with him. The Angel agreed, but said he was broke. No sweat, Charlie said. They'd hitch-hike and if he needed bread, he'd lend it to him. It was an offer the Angel, wise in such Godsent things, couldn't refuse.

The trip took three days, and from what the Angel says, every minute of it was a high. They got rides from nymphomaniacs and millionaires. When they got to D.C., they stayed at a commune run by a friend of his. Abbie Hoffman came over and Abbie and Charlie flashed on each other. Instant groove! Abbie was very busy, but when the Angel called him he said he'd drop everything, since he hadn't seen his old stickball pal in years. Charlie told him he couldn't thank him enough for meeting Abbie. What the fuck, the Angel said, he was happy to set it up. Blah blah blah.

When Charlie got back to the square, he said it rained all the while and they got drenched. They got picked up by a faggot who tried to put the make on him. The Angel made a phone call when they got to D.C. and asked to borrow $50 for his sister, strung-out on smack. Charlie wanted to meet his junkie-sister but the Angel said he couldn't take him because it was too sickening. The Angel changed his mind at the last minute about Abbie. Abbie was too busy writing a speech and he didn't want to disturb him. The Revolution was more important, the Angel said.

It was such a bummer, Charlie said, he spent most of his time touring, seeing Nixon's White House and the monuments. They slept in a flophouse where Charlie got up in the middle of the night and bumped into a guy strolling the corridor stark naked except for a shoulder holster. It was such a bummer they hitched back to Missouri as fast as they could.

Charlie didn't go to Lawrence after that and the Angel didn't make any more regal appearances on the square. Charlie didn't talk much about him. Two or three times he said he was going to go up to Lawrence to get his money from the candy-snake sonofabitch, but somehow he never did that, either. "You can't trust anybody," he told Rise, "only yourself."

IT snowed hard that winter and they abandoned their outdoor amphitheater and set up a commune. It was a rickety Victorian house that hadn't been used since its last tenant, who worked at the Chevy plant in Raytown, came home from the assembly line, splattered his wife's henpecking face all over the kitchen wall, and stuck his head into the oven. Gas didn't do the job; the man had to use the shotgun on himself. He did, and missed. Luckily, he died a week later of further complications.

The house was owned by one of the richest men in town, whose son dropped out of school and started hanging around the square. The kid asked to use the Murder House and his father indignantly refused. No son of his was going to live in homo wedlock with a bunch of hippies. Fine, the kid said, he was leaving for San Francisco. His father changed his mind. It was a perfect arrangement. Bill Davis's cops parked across the street in shifts but were afraid to bust them because the kid's father had too much civic clout. They were turning the System they despised against itself.

Charlie didn't live there; he stayed overnight sometimes and brought them bread and donuts. The delivery truck came to Lane's IGA Foodlane in Holden just after cockcrow each day and left its goodies piled high against the backdoor. Charlie kypped a few loaves of bread and boxes of donuts and never got caught. When he walked into the Murder House, they jibed: "The bread-man's here!"

His Bros loved him. Harry Miller says: "He was full of feelings, just look at his face and you could tell. Just look at his face and you'd say—'Man, that guy there, he'll give me a dollar to get something to eat.' Anytime somebody was depressed, he was around to help the guy out. His feelings were so sensitive, like, you couldn't gross him out, but he had such feelings for his friends. He could stand fifty feet away and somebody would jump on you and the vibes from Ootney would knock you down. If we were having a hassle, fucking Ootney would pick up the vibes thirty miles away. He changed everyday. Like, he might be growing his beard and then one day he'd say—'Fuck it, man, I'm tired of the way I look, I'm gonna cut it.' We tried to gross him out about it, saying—'You're too much of a pussy bastard to grow a beard, you're scared of what the fucking women are gonna say,' and he'd just laugh and smile, dance around."

Rise says: "If he felt like taking off his clothes, he didn't give a fuck who was there, no, he'd take his clothes off and take a bath or something. He was a peach, true beautifulness. He was a freak, a real freak all the way. When he let his beard grow, the only thing you could see was the eyes—just the whites of 'em, 'cause the rest of him was dark. He was a real killer, man."

The breadman who was a real killer served as the Murder House's enforcer. Whenever there was a hassle, Charlie Simpson got into it and, bang!, no more hassle.

One night a friend of theirs, gigglewatered and ornery, invited a United States Marine Corps Vietnam veteran to the hippies' Murder House. The Marine was fifteen beers to the wind. When he stepped inside and saw the posters of Che and Easy Rider and the length of Rise Risner's hair, the Marine said: "Goddamn, you don't fight for your country, you oughtta be shot!"

"Ootney heard it," Harry Miller says. "This guy was gonna fire on Rise's ass. Ootney gets up stark naked, walks in there, and comes down into shit like Rubin jumping a Chicago pig's ass or something. And jumps all over the Marine. He looks the dude back about three steps and he grabs his prick and shakes it at the Marine and turns around and just shoots him the moon and then gives him the finger. Man, that Marine, he ran away!"

His brother, Bub, started coming to the Murder House, too. He left his cold-creamed wife and, hip deep in bills, hung around with Charlie. One day Charlie, Win, Rise, and a few of their Bros escorted Bub to the Holden Courthouse. Bub was charged with disturbing the peace, riding his motorcycle up and down Locust Street.

The judge found Bub guilty. Win, dressed in his dashiki and wearing a Jimi Hendrix frowsy-headed supernigger wig, yelled: "Bullshit!"

The judge called him to the bench.

"Do you know the prior defendant?" he asked.

"Yeah, I know him," Win said, "he's a citizen of America."

The judge fined him $50 for contempt of court. Win was broke, headed once again for the monkeybars. One of Applesauce Wakeman's policemen grabbed his arm and said: "Boy, come along with me!"

("Boy, dig?" Win says, "I was gonna slide with it.")

Charlie said: "Stop the music, I'll pay the Nigger's fine."

("They freaked out," Win says, "they didn't know how to react. They smiled.")

Charlie paid the $50 and said: "We'll teach the Nigger a lesson once we get him into his cage."

("Sheeit," Win says, "we laughed all the way out of town. The judge must've thought Ootney was gonna cut my prick off and put it down my throat or something.")

As the weather warmed, he talked more and more about the

rockhouse he'd build on his plot of land. "I'm gonna live like old Toe-Row," he said, "fuck all you longhaired hippie dudes." They saw him, too, with a new squirrel gun, a carbine which left gaping holes in the trees. No big thing, he said, a gift from a friend . . . but it was a lie.

THE gun was a .30 caliber Universal M–1 carbine, serial number 177729. He bought it on the 14th of December from Paul Smith, of Grandview, who grew up with him. Smith's wife worked at a gunshop in Kansas City and was entitled to a 50 percent employee's discount. Charlie got his cutrate M–1 for $55. He said he needed it to shoot targets.

He tested the gun in the fields and it was during one of these outings, in nearby Henry County, that he found his plot of land. It was barren, filled with lime and sandstone, ideal for building his rockhouse. There was no pond, but its thirteen acres were surrounded by thickets of wild plum and groves of crabapples. He drove Rise and Win out there, on a dirtroad shouldered by boulders, and said: "Welcome to my land." Charlie talked about the Osage Indians.

Toe-Row would have dug the Osage; Charlie said he'd live like them. They were tall robust wide-shouldered, swift in their movements, and said little. They walked sixty miles to a trading post, bore sickness and pain with sufferance and fortitude, kept time by the waxing and waning of the moon. They built their lodges the way he'd build his rockhouse. They staked twenty-foot poles into the earth and covered the walls with a matting of rushes. Fires were built in the center of the lodge; smokeholes carved into the matting. A sixfoot bearskin platform was their place for Bros and wise men.

"It's a shitty piece of land," Rise said, "rocks and more fucking rocks, real freak's land. You think the neck's gonna sell it to you?"

"Sure," he said, "I got the bread."

The owner was a redneck farmer a mile away who took one look at him and said: "You ain't got enough money to buy it."

Charlie sweet-talked him. He told him about growing up on a farm, about loving his blackland and his chores. He told him he'd dreamed about owning a plot of land like this one. The redneck said he'd think it over.

He went back three days later and the redneck said: "How come your hair's so long?"

Charlie said he liked it that way.

"I don't want a company of hippies carrying on out here," the farmer said.

Charlie said he'd live there alone with the sun and the stars and the waxing and waning of the moon.

"How much can you pay?" the farmer asked.

"How much you want?"

"How much is it worth to you?"

It was worth his lifesavings: $1,500.

"Yeah," the farmer said, "I reckon I'll sell it to you."

Forms and papers had to be filled out. The farmer had to talk to his lawyer, who had to draw up a deed, which had to be sent to the capital, Jefferson City.

Charlie went back two weeks later and the farmer still hadn't talked to his lawyer.

He went back after another week and the lawyer still hadn't drawn up the deed.

He went back after two more weeks, certain now the farmer's lawyer had had enough time, telling Rise and Win they could help him gather the rocks for his house.

"There's too much redtape," the farmer said. "I don't want to sell it to no hippie anyway. Hell with it!"

He was heartbroken and angry. He told Bub it was a ruse. The redneck wanted to screw more money out of him, wanted to be begged and asslicked with more cash. He told Rise he felt like blowing his brains out, "ending it." Rise told him he was crazy to let one fractious redneck twist his head up that bad. There were millions of rocks all over Missouri, thousands of farmers willing to sell land they couldn't use.

"What's the use?" Charlie said.

A high school buddy, Mike Young, saw him for a few minutes on the square.

"How you doing?" Mike asked.

"I'm sick of the world," Charlie said, "but it's nothing serious."

Mike Young noticed that Charlie was crying.

He took his $55 M–1 down to the Osage riverbank, once the Indians' hunting ground, and slept there that night. "The only time I feel like a natural person," he'd told Rise, "is when I'm down by the river alone." It was Wednesday, the 19th of April, forty-eight hours from the last time Charlie Simpson shot targets.

ON Friday morning, he stopped off at home on the way from the bank to the sheriff's office and said he was using all his saved-up money to bail his Bros out of jail.

The ashen-faced old man sitting in the roominghouse said: "What about the land?"

"It don't matter now," Charlie told his father.

Charles B. Simpson is fifty-three years old and appears seventy-five. He looks like a man who is going to die and has looked that way for years. His face is emaciated, his nose starkly aquiline, his eyes pooled by liverish scoops. He stands 6 foot 2, weighs a little more than 150 pounds, sports a red five-and-dime baseball cap and a cardigan which has fed too many moths. He walks with face-twisted pain and a briar walking stick with vulcanized rubbertip. He was shot apart on the European front in World War II.

The corpse-faced war-vet and his oldest boy were never too close and it was only in the past few years they did any talking. It was hard for the old man to get around and he spent long hours cogitating in his rockingchair, in the room with the calico rug and the calendar filled with bone-chilling winterset scenes. He sat pegrocking in the chair, the baseball cap pulled over eyes the color of twilight, the cane draped over a thigh, staring at the cracked-plaster walls and the dates on the calendar, pouring himself a bracer of sink-taller whiskey now and then. The boy would wander in, long hippie hair in his face, and they'd talk. They talked about the land, the crops, and war, about policemen, guns, and steer, about Henry David Toe-Row, Abbie Hoffman, and General of the Army Douglas MacArthur.

He was alway filling the old man full of Henry David Toe-Row. How he took long walks in the woods. How his friends were plants, animals, and the wilderness. How he wouldn't pay his taxes. How he felt he had to speak up against injustice. How he was somebody you could believe in.

The old man didn't have too much to say about Henry David Toe-Row, but a man talking to his son has to have something to say, so he told the boy stories about General Douglas MacArthur. How General MacArthur won the Philippines from the Japs. How he could have beat the Chinee across the Yaloo River if Harry S Truman hadn't stopped him. How Harry S Truman once wanted to be a piano player in a joyhouse and that's where he belonged. How General Douglas MacArthur should have been President of these United States and we wouldn't be in the fix we're in.

The old man didn't exactly know what the boy did in Harrisonville all the time (he didn't like a lot of what he heard), but he did know policemen didn't much like him. Applesauce Wakeman came over one day with a flame up his fat ass and told him to keep his damn boy out of his hair. The old man figured the police were getting a rise out of stopping his son and he told Charlie: "They figure you're always good for a $100 fine. You talk about law and order, hell, there's too much law and not enough order."

He tried to talk some sense into the boy but most of the time Charlie laughed at him like a flapjack ninny. "Cut your hair," he told him, "get a burrcut like when you were in high school and these police won't be picking on you all the time." Charlie said: "I can't get it cut. It's one of the few freedoms I got left."

Or like the time they stopped the boy in Kingsville for driving a car with loud pipes. The policeman told him to step on the gas so he could hear the pipes. Charlie stuck the accelerator to the floorboard; the policeman gave him a ticket. He refused to sign it and wound up in jail.

"You proved nothing but your mule-headedness," the old man told him.

When Charlie said: "One of these days I'm not gonna let 'em push me around," the old man replied: "You can't settle jackshit with violence."

Charlie was bitter about richfolks' kids getting away with everything and the old man couldn't argue that. "It's always been like that," he told him, "it's always gonna be like that."

"Everybody's phony," the boy said, "nobody gives a shit whether you live or die," and his father said yeah, that's life allright. They'd never had it easy, bouncing from farm to farm and then to the sparsely furnished rooms in a roominghouse while richfolks lived in $150,000 mansions with twenty-five rooms.

He asked the boy if he'd ever get married and Charlie said: "Yeah, but not in this kind of world."

When Charlie didn't heed what he told him, the old man read him the Lord's commandment: "Honor thy father and thy mother."

And Charlie said: "That means honor thy Father in heaven and Mother Earth."

They tried to talk about things they agreed on, like George C. Wallace. The old man thought George C. Wallace was the redeemer of this screwed-up country and the boy said he'd vote for George C. Wallace because he didn't sling any shit and because "he'll bring things to a head quicker."

So they lived in their decrepit few rooms, father and son, war-vet and revolutionary, and killed time together. The war-vet stared at the calendar and the revolutionary waited for apocalypse and they both went to the same bank with their government paychecks. The war-vet got paid for his infirmity and the revolutionary for his idleness.

That Friday, after he bailed his Bros out of the crabseat, Charlie went back to the house and got his semiautomatic M–1.

"What you taking the gun for?" the old man asked.

"Gonna shoot me some targets," the boy said, "good day for squirrels." He walked out and that was it . . . never even said goodbye.

FROM the State of Missouri Highway Patrol Supplementary Investigation Report, page six. Subject: Charles Simpson, deceased. Nature of crime: homicide:

"The reporting officer contacted Charles B. Simpson, age 53, and Elwin K. Simpson, Bub, age 23, at their home in Holden, Mo. Both persons were polite and cooperative with this officer. Due to the noise from a chainsaw in the yard, they preferred to talk with me in the patrol car.

"While both persons indicated they were ready to talk about Charles Simpson, Bub said he probably knew and understood Charles the best and the father agreed.

"Charles and Bub's interest was mainly centered on their cars and racing until 1970. After he quit racing Charles Simpson took an interest in revolutionary literature and ecology (no attempt was made to learn the connection between the two interests). Charles read works from Thoreau and also read Eldridge Cleaver, Abbie Hoffman, and others. He often read the Kansas-City Star. He became convinced from reading these things that the only way for social reorganization was by violence and revolution.

"Mr. Simpson indicated here that Charles fancied himself a leader among his friends. He said he believed the friends capitalized on this desire by placing Charles in front when they were in trouble, or when they wanted to start trouble. I asked Bub Simpson if he knew for a fact that acts of fornication had taken place on the courthouse lawn in daylight in Harrisonville. He did not deny it and would not admit having seen this or participated. However he hesitated a long time before answering. Mr. Simpson said he had heard enough that he believed it and had told the boys to follow the Lord's commandments.

"The Simpsons agreed with each other that the killing of the police officers and his own act of suicide were acts of rebellion that had been characteristic of Charles for some time. They had not believed he would go this far and did not believe he was rational when the shooting occurred.

"When asked directly by this officer as to why this happened in Harrisonville, both men agreed that it 'just happened there. It could just as well have been Holden, Kingsville, or any place.'

"The Simpsons were quiet, cooperative, and polite in talking with this officer. They talked freely and openly. The interview flowed so smoothly that under the circumstances I was somewhat concerned about it."

Attached to the report was a paperback found in the deceased's room— *Woodstock Nation,* by Abbie Hoffman. On page 133, these sentences were underlined:

"When you learn to survive in a hostile environment, be it the tear gas parks of Chicago or the mud slopes of WOODSTOCK NATION, you learn a little more of the universal puzzle, you learn a little more about yourself, and you learn about the absurdity of any analysis at all. It's only when you get to the End of Reason can you begin to enter WOODSTOCK NATION."

ON his body they found:

*A three-inch black Boy Scout knife with rusted blade and elastic handle, one of its sides missing.

*A Holden Farmers and Commercial bankbook showing a withdrawal of $1,550 from a savings account on April 21st. Balance: $25.00.

*Two mimeographed leaflets to be distributed at the antiwar rally on the square Saturday, April 22nd. The leaflets said:

STOP THE WAR!

With the Vietnam War now past its tenth year, it is quite clear that the Nixon Administration has no intention of ending it. The time has come for every citizen to exercise his freedom of speech and speak out loudly aganst the war and all other suppressions in the United States of America. No person who claims to be a human being can justify the napalming and bombing of small children, women, and men. It is quite clear now that the war serves no purpose other than to make wealthy people richer, at the expense of the poor's sons and taxes. American youth has deeply rooted emotions against the bombing and the war. Your tax dollars are paying for the unimaginable expenses of these atrocities, and if you give a damn about your earth, children, and selves, speak out now. STOP THE BOMBING AND THE WAR NOW!

POLICE BRUTALITY!
HARRISONVILLE POLICE UNFAIR TO AREA YOUTH!

Discrimination in any form is immoral and unconstitutional. But the absurdity in which the Harrisonville Police Department is exercising its powers is inhumane, unfair, biased, and cruel. The town merchants of Harrisonville act as if they are the only ones paying taxes in the city. They have total control of the Harrisonville Police Department and are forcing them to discriminate against all youth. A town merchant started a fight with a young man on the square, the police came and immediately started clubbing the young man, tightly handcuffed him and arrested him while the merchant was allowed to go free. Several other youths were arrested and beaten by the Harrisonville Police Department who do not have the intelligence to understand the constitutional rights of people and especially public property. You are urged to go to City Hall, read the new ordinances passed and protest them and reprimand the city council strongly.

These ordinances are in strong conflict with the Constitutional rights of all citizens and are aimed at and enforced on only a certain group. This is not fair and the Harrisonville Police Department docs not have the intelligence to know what they are doing. As a concerned citizen you should protest these ordinances now. They concern your children and their physical safety. ACT NOW!

* Three full 30–round clips for a Universal .30 caliber carbine. One 30–round clip with 29 rounds. One full fifteen round clip. 234 live rounds loose in jacket pockets.

* Five nickels, one dime.

III
Fire on the Prairie

IN *the days of wilderness, before the sky was filled with poisons and the food with rathairs, prairie grass grew as high as a strapping man's bellybutton. The tallgrass needed rainwater to live, and when the sunball blasted the prairie dry and flammable as tinder, the wildfire came. The air was a filmy haze and at night the horizon was fringed with pale red tints that jumped into forked flames. If a wind gusted, the flames raced and jitterbugged across the land, blotting the sun with smoke and lighting the sky with ashes and flying sparks. Everything burned . . . until the last tuft of withered grass was scorched, or until it rained. No living creature could endure such travail and the riverbanks were strewn with animals howling in panic and pain.*

In the summer of 1972 the sunball blazed and the rain avoided Harrisonville. The grass was parched and dry, a place only of pollutants, waste, and bugdust. Tomatoes, known as love apples, wilted, their foliage yellow and limp, their stems a scabrous brown. Shade trees and shrubs drooped with leafscorch; denied water, the tips of leaves turned the no-color of cardboard.

The land was plagued. Temperatures ranged from the high 90s to 104. It rained .12 of an inch in June, a month the normal precipitation is four inches. The corn was tasseling and needed one good goose-drowning downpour to stay alive, but the infinitesimal amount of rainfall did it no good. It was a hard-driving shower that skittered off and didn't penetrate the soil. Crops were burning to

/ 131

death and farmers stayed in their fields, weapons in hand, to fight the sun. One of their weapons was a traveling gun. Hooked to a waterline, it shot two inches of water a day on twenty-five acres.

On an afternoon in June when it was 102 degrees, a northbound freight crawling along the Missouri-Pacific tracks sparked a grassfire. Flames leaped through the tallgrass less than a mile from town; the Volunteer Fire Department mobilized its vehicles, including brush-buggy and tanker. The blaze spread like a wildfire, licking at the shoulders of a blacktop road. The wind kicked up and thick black smoke drifted across the town and its square. The brush-buggy did its robotized job and in three hours the grassfire—which tried to be a wildfire—was dead.

THEY tried to pick up the pieces . . .

The merchants in the stores around the square pretended they were a shopping center; they called their shops "Square Center" and promoted a "Moonlight Madness Sale." Prizes were awarded to customers "best-dressed for moonlight activity." They held a festival on the four streets surrounding the courthouse, with entertainment by the Boy Scout Drum and Bugle Corps, and featuring carnival rides like the Zipper! the Tempest! and the Tilt!

The Allen Bank and Trust Company, bulletholes still in its walls, announced it was moving off the square to South Commercial Street, within easy access of I–71. The Band-Aides, parents whose kids played in the high school band, asked the community to buy their teenagers new $115 uniforms complete with white spats and gloves, washable tophats, blue bowties, and purple trousers. The Cass County Barbershop Quartet singers fulfilled the lofty requirements of the International Society for the Preservation and Encouragement of Barbershop Singing in America and were granted a local chapter. A Paint Horse Show was held at the Peculiar Rodeo Grounds; Dr. G.G. Kroenke, of Harrisonville, showed off Blasting Cap, his prize sorrel tobiano stallion.

The fishing season began in earnest and the *Democrat-Missourian* ran a three-column picture, taken forty years ago, of a man in porkpie hat waving a fat seven-pound bass, with the cutline: "The Good Old Days weren't so bad, were they?" A welder snagged a record muskie with a ten-pound line and crappie jig; his wife ran to a store and bought a net while the welder battled the fish. The turkey season was in full strutting gear: an eight-year-old boy, kneehigh to a Junebug, bagged a twenty-six-pound gobbler at seventeen steps; the conservation agent was called out three times to remove hardheaded wild hen turks which squatted in front of bulldozers and refused to let them gobble the land.

Ladies busied themselves. The Harrisonville Ladies Softball Team lost its biggest game—to the ladies from Rich Hill, 12–10. The Harrisonville ladies scored four runs in the first inning, thanks to a homerun blasted by a cashier at G.M. Allen's bank. But, alas, the ladies dropped three easy Texas-leaguer popflies. A waitress at the Harrisonville Hotel pitched. She struckout four, walked eight, and beaned two. The Mary Sibley chapter of the Daughters of the American Revolution increased its members to twenty-three and won two DAR contests: for highest percentage of DAR magazine subscriptions in the nation and the largest membership increase in the state. A dewlap-necked DAR housewife sewed an American flag for the blind; each of the flag's colors was of different-textured material.

City Council urged a drive "to interest our young people in healthy pursuits, such as the Boy and Girl Scout programs." Four scouts qualified for God and Country Awards; twenty-four were driven to Colorado Springs, Colo., where they toured the U.S. Air Force Academy and ate a sloppyjoe lunch in the Airmen's Dining Hall. The Girl Scouts awarded a certificate of appreciation to G.M. Allen's Citizens National Bank for a $50 donation and planned a Poppy Day Sale for the American Legion Auxiliary. A Cass County "Sing Out" group was formed; under contract to "Up With People," its goal was "to bring a message of patriotism and peace." J.W. Brown wrote an editorial in the *Democrat-Missourian* urging businessmen to hire some of the 675 recent high school graduates and punchlined: "Let's not let Cass County's greatest asset, its youth, slip through our fingers."

It was a banner summer for G.M. Allen. His bank merged with Commerce Bancshares of Kansas City and G.M. humbly declared: "This solid, seventy-year-old bank, appreciating the confidence and trust of each one of its thousands of valued customers, will continue to provide personal attention in a friendly atmosphere and feel confident the people in the surrounding area will join the staff in anticipation of this latest progressive development." G.M.'s son, Nelson, an attorney with the town's most prestigious lawfirm, married a cutesy schoolteacher with cherrylips and Pepsodent smile. The organist played "Theme from 'Love Story'" and the bride carried a cascade bouquet of white roses, stephanotis, and baby's-breath.

The Chamber of Commerce announced Harrisonville was officially entered in the *Saturday Evening Post*'s "All-America City" contest. The winner would be selected on the basis of "strong citizen action toward improving quality of life and action creating conditions which provide a better life for residents of a community."

Runnenburger's Funeral Home ran a new obit-bordered ad in the *Democrat-Missourian:*

TO OUR NEWER RESIDENTS!

Welcome to our town. We hope you have come to know and enjoy the warm feeling of friendship and pleasant living that has always been part of our community. You will likewise come to know those businesses in our community which over the years have, through their policies of service and integrity, helped build and strengthen this community. We are proud to have been a part of this progress and pledge our continued policy of complete service at a cost within reach of all.

AS much as they tried to forget, to hide the blood under the civic rug, it seemed wellnigh impossible. The hippies were still on the square, still hurling Frisbees, obscenities, and insults, still waving clenched fists to the sky. They camped up there with their wine, their skunks, and their Nigger, and poked fun at them right over those three dead bodies.

Everett Wade, the turtle-headed juvenile officer, advised the aldermen of the putrefaction which smelled up his files . . . A black baby was born to a goldilocked high school senior . . . Another seventeen-year-old gal, one of the hippies' hussies, was jazzed-up, and Everett Wade was dutybound to send her to a home because her parents said they couldn't do anything with her. The girl called her own parents pigs and accused her father, her own flesh and blood, of trying to cabbage onto her . . . The courthouse groundskeeper still collected souvenirs; one day the man brought Everett Wade a tiny box filled with high velocity .22 bullets.

Everett Wade also said some of the delinquents he interviewed told him Charlie Simpson was part of a conspiracy that never got off the ground. Simpson's volley was supposed to trigger sniperfire from all over the square, but the yellahdog hippies didn't have the stuffings to finish the job they'd suckered Simpson into. Some of the aldermen, like seventy-ish Felix Hacker, a retired preacher who keeps the Book of Mormon open on his desk, swallowed the conspiracy talk and pinned the blame on Cass County prosecutor Don Whitcraft. Whitcraft wasn't one of their own: he lived in Belton, he used to be a kingshit lawyer in Kansas City, he fast-talked and backslapped like a coffin salesman, he liked to be seen jawing with Win Allen, and he got a convenient heart attack a few weeks after the shooting. Don Whitcraft, Hacker and some of the aldermen charged, whitewashed the hippies just to avoid headaches and paperwork.

Whitcraft heard the talk and told the aldermen they were crazy. He is a reedy irongray haggard man whose heart attack has forced him to chew unlighted cigars. "We had thirteen FBI men in here," he says. "The FBI came in because Simpson shot up the bank and that gives the FBI the excuse—I mean, the right—to investigate. We had dozens of highway patrolmen. It was their joint conclusion there was no conspiracy. My God, all those guys were hoping for, dreaming about a conspiracy. A couple of their own got killed—by a longhair. It just defies any kind of thinking that cops, having a shot at a conspiracy involving a copkiller-hippie, wouldn't give it two hundred percent."

The aldermen ignored Don Whitcraft's denials and said he was posturing, washing his hands. G.M. Allen and Mayor Raine, who once had bootlick ties to Kansas City's Byzantine political machine, called their congressman in Washington, the Hon. William J. Randall, Democrat, member of the Armed Services Committee, and asked for help. Sure, said Bill Randall, a few months from a tough election, he'd be happy to help. The congressman came all the way from the United States capital to the Harrisonville City Hall just to listen to the aldermen's woes.

Bill Randall, smooth and urbane, blessed with a pragmatic allpurpose folksiness usually kept in the closet, was well groomed for the meeting. He'd just finished polling the citizens of Cass County. He knew that 79 percent of voting Cass residents favored increased spending to control crime and narcotics; 91 percent insisted on work requirements for all able-bodied welfare recipients under the age of sixty-five; 61 percent supported the War in Vietnam; only 3 percent supported amnesty for draft evaders.

The aldermen detailed their woes: Newspaper reporters from the *Kansas City Star* were bloodhounding through town each day, writing sobsister sensation-seeking accounts favorable to the hippies . . . Unemployment compensation was available to "all the undesirable elements" and the government was actually financing the manhours spent plotting a mass-murdering revolution . . . Commodity foods were available to the unemployed longhairs and their own taxdollars went to feed scum who were shooting them down . . . The Supreme Court was a tool of these revolutionaries, giving them counsel and, as Chief Davis said, virtual sanctuary.

Bill Randall, a clever politician, said: "I've always admired the straight-thinking viewpoints expressed by you fine people in America's heartland." He told them Harrisonville's symptoms were part of a national malaise. He reviewed proposed legislation which would be crime-deterrent and said he backed that legislation "body and soul." He urged those who knew of welfare abuses to do something about it.

"What?" someone asked him.

"Write a letter to the director of the Missouri Welfare Department," the congressman said.

When they told him about the conspiracy and their mealy-mouthed county prosecutor's refusal to see it, Bill Randall said he'd hurry back to Washington and have the FBI look into it. They thanked him profusely for coming all the way from Washington to listen to them and promised to remember his visit in November. The congressman left in a halo of conviviality, nicotine, and hot air.

Even as Don Whitcraft continued to insist a conspiracy was hogwash, Felix Hacker talked to Bill Randall on the telephone.

It was true, the congressman said. They were right. There was a conspiracy, but the FBI couldn't come up with the goods to prove it. Felix Hacker told the other aldermen what the congressman had said (the Hon. William J. Randall would later deny it) and council demanded a special grand jury. Don Whitcraft, who'd left Kansas City because he tired of the ratrace and wanted solace, said no. Absolutely not. He would not permit a pack of redeyed amateur DA's to waste the taxpayers' money and go howling up a tree trying to hang people for something that never happened. There would be no grand jury, Don Whitcraft said, because there was no conspiracy. Period.

They were frustrated and afraid that Charlie Simpson's gunfire would somehow sully all their acehigh reputations. There was even an editorial in the Bates County *News Headliner* that said: "Three innocent people were assassinated on the streets of Harrisonville recently but Cass County and its fine people are not to be written off as outcasts. Decent citizens deplore such acts of violence and are surely not to be blamed for the crazed minority whose only way of life is violence." The aldermen wanted to take some sort of action to rid the town of its killer longhairs, but what more could they do? Letters were coming in from all over the country *blaming them*, telling them they had to do something, letters like the one sent to the Chamber of Commerce.

> Gentlemen:
> You and your town have paid the price for not cleaning your streets and schools when they should have been. Please learn from your mistake. Give the authority to your civil workers and direct your school officials to take prompt action whenever needed and back their actions 100%. Give them assurance. Your stern actions can teach our nation a lesson which it badly needs. We have scoundrels, hippies, and drugs because we allow them to be.
> God help you,
> A parent of children

At the same time, the Rev. W.T. Niermeier, of Our Savior Lutheran Church, who'd buried Don Marler's blown-apart body, was interpreting the relationship of the Word of God to events in Harrisonville. "We drastically need a return to the rule of law," the reverend wrote in the *Democrat-Missourian*, "law based on the moral laws laid down and backed by the power of God . . . It would be difficult to think of a more disastrous way for our Supreme Court to celebrate the 196th birthday of our nation than by taking steps to eliminate the death penalty. To call the death penalty cruel is to fly in the face of God . . . The young generations' deterioration of morals and the abrogation of moral laws is being taught and promoted."

Morals were being destroyed and laws abrogated right in their once-smiling faces, day after day. And what did they do about it? Lament their murdered dead, sit on their hindsides talking about conspiracy and doing scratch about it? The Chamber of Commerce had just scheduled a special meeting with the City Council when they got kicked in the teeth again. The Nigger was cleared! The Supreme Court-subverted system of law found the criminal innocent once again.

The charge stretched back to the day before the shooting when, after the fight with Sears-store-owner Don Foster, Win Allen was charged with resisting arrest and kicking a police officer. The judge said that if a struggle did occur, it was after the arrest. Allen couldn't be found guilty of resisting during the arrest. The aldermen and many of the townspeople were furious. The judge found the hippies guilty of disturbing the peace during the same incident, but that was a dingleberry charge. It was a misdemeanor; they'd get $50 fines and couldn't be locked in jail. And they were already talking to one of those jackleg civil liberties lawyers about appealing to a higher court, which meant they'd probably get off clean as a hound's tooth.

The answer, many people in Harrisonville felt, wasn't to take these longhairs to court; they'd only be set free and sugar-taffied in the *Kansas City Star*. The answer was what Gene Kane, a farmer, did over in Holden. One of Simpson's longhaired friends was monkeying with Gene Kane's car and he shot the eighteen-year-old boy in the face with a .410 shotgun blast. The hippie was charged with "tampering with a motor vehicle." He was alive, but he couldn't see too well.

After weighty deliberation, the City Council did three things: it participated in a Youth Crime Conference at the University of Missouri; it endorsed a state senator's proposal to form the Missouri Bureau of Investigation, a mini-FBI; and, together with the Chamber of Commerce, it held a posh Appreciation Dinner and handed out a batch of plaques.

Recognized for their "devotion to duty and efforts to keep the peace" in the days after the shooting were: G.M. Allen, Sheriff Gough, Police Chief Davis, Mayor Raine, the entire City Council, and George Van Antwerp, "unsung hero," who drove the ambulance around the square. Sears-store-owner Don Foster was appointed one of the Chamber's board members.

As far as an increasing number of townspeople were concerned, the aldermen and Chamber of Commerce members did nothing but keep their thumbs firmly up their portholes. The townspeople knew only that the Nigger and his longhairs were still desecrating their bloodied streets . . . Chief Davis's men were taking extra target-practice on a mobile range carted down from Kansas City . . . mysterious revolutionaries prowled their highways bragging that more people were going to die.

"**MY** name is Richard Earl Johnson. I am eighteen years old and I work at the Hamins DX gas station on No. 7 Highway outside Harrisonville.

"I was working about 5:30 one night when these boys came in and they was driving a 1962 or 1963 Ford Mercury. There were three men in it and this old boy, the driver of the car. He got out and was asking all about where a couple of girls lived and Dan Hamins, who runs the station, lipped off to him about the way he came into the drive. He got all started on that and then he started talking about if we knew Simpson and all and Dan said —'Well, you mean the boy that blew off his head in Harrisonville?' and the old boy got all hacked off and he goes—'Well, it's not all over with!'

"He turned around and he started saying he had a 30-ott carbine out in the car and he says—'Do you want me to get it for you?' and Dan goes—'Naw' and the guy goes—'Well, I'll get it out and show it to you!' And about this time I started to walk inside and get me a pack of cigarettes and this old boy he grabbed ahold of my arm and jerked me back and said—'You're not going to spend 10 cents on my pair of 49-cent socks!' I don't know what that meant, I guess he thought I'd use the phone or something to call the cops and he got all mad about that.

"They also said that they had got their hair cut so that they wouldn't be recognized and so they'd have an equal chance to do whatever they wanted to get done. They said that they was going to finish the policemen up in Harrisonville, and the only reason they didn't get another policeman was he got off duty. But this old boy said that he was going to finish the job up that Simpson was starting to do. And then he said—'Well, after we get done over there, it's going to be Pleasant Hill's turn!' I was really scared to move or anything but he said something about—'Well, tomorrow's my birthday and it's Pleasant Hill's turn.' When this old boy started talking about all this, the other guys in the car got all mad about it and this other guy scooted over behind the wheel and he started to drive. And this old boy goes—'Well, if he don't come back I'm not worried about it 'cause I'll shoot him and anybody else that gets in my path.' The car took off down the road and this guy says—'Well, those sons of bitches, they'll be back 'cause they know that if they don't, I'll kill 'em.' Then the car came back and the other guys were laughing and this old boy gets in and they took off. That was about the last we seen of them."

My name is Don Hamins. I am fifty-nine years old and I own and operate the Hamins DX gas station and car wash on No. 7 Highway outside Harrisonville.

"A blue Mercury pulled into my place, swung around, and liked to turn over, and they pulled on up to the store. The boy that jumped out was bung-eyed drunk, I could see that rightoff. I asked him—'What are you trying to prove? Do you get fever with them spells?' He said—'Do you want to come out here and take my temperature?' I said—'No, I don't want to take your temperature.' He said—'Well, I'll let you know right now we're followers of Simpson and this matter isn't over yet. We've cleaned up and we've shaved off and we're going over to Harrisonville where we can get in, because we couldn't get in with the longhair that we had. But the first thing we're going to do is . . . there are two of them over there who are going to get it. One of them is the sheriff and the other is the deputy sheriff and after we get through with 'em we're going to clean Pleasant Hill out, too.' So I didn't say anything when I seen he was drunk and finally he cooled down a little and he asked where some girls lived. He said —'I'm going over there and rape them two girls over there.' "

My name is Bill Hamins. I am thirty-one years old and I work at my dad's DX gas station outside Harrisonville.

"I'd just come from eating supper and I got out of the truck and walked into the store and noticed the car. It looked like there were about three guys in the car. One guy standing out in front of the store talking to my dad and Dickie Johnson, who works in the store. I didn't know just what exactly was going on at the time. I noticed after I got inside the store this fellow seemed to be pretty lathered up, drugged or something, using foul language, particularly aiming most of it at my dad. I sat down in the chair there and started listening to it a little bit and I heard this fella talking about how he was one of Simpson's buddies. Simpson was his hero and he was talking about how they took Simpson's life away from him and how he was gonna get even with the police. I was starting to get a little mad about this deal and then I heard him mention about how he had a 30-caliber carbine in the car and I wasn't armed or nothing, and I thought—Well, under the circumstances, I'd just better set back and play it by ear 'cause I figured I didn't have much of a chance against an automatic carbine.

"Anyway, I stood there and listened to him some more and he said they were going over to somebody's house and rape a couple of gals. I heard him say a thing or two in particular. I heard him say they were going to get Bill Gough, the sheriff, and the deputy and when they were done killing they'd go and kill the Pleasant Hill police."

My name is Junior Lawrence. I am twenty-nine years old and

I work for the Pleasant Hill Police Department.

"We got a call from the Hamins gas station about some boys threatening to kill all the police and a couple minutes after that I got a call about a drunk up on North Campbell. I went up there and this drunk was walking toward me and I picked him up and he said somebody stole his car. It was a 1964 Mercury, four-door blue hardtop with Iowa plates. Chief Daugherty was working on an accident, so I took him up there and the chief took him down to City Hall and questioned him."

My name is Hershel Daugherty. I am fifty-six years old. I am the police chief of Pleasant Hill, Missouri.

"I got in the car with Officer Lawrence and the subject he had picked up and we came to police headquarters. The subject identified himself as Paul Sam Pollard, DOB Feb. 15, 1940, address, Route #2, Holden. He said that he came to Pleasant Hill with three other subjects, also of Holden. He said that he met these three other subjects in the afternoon in a beerjoint in Holden and they got together and came up this way in Pollard's automobile. Subject wasn't too intoxicated that he didn't know what he was saying or doing. He didn't seem to be in too bad shape.

"He said that the three other subjects had kicked him out of his car and taken his car and he wanted to go home. He told us that these three other subjects had said their job wasn't finished yet. He said that the shooting that occurred in Harrisonville . . . that they did not get one officer they intended to get because he had just gone off duty and that they got Officer Wirt by mistake . . . so they still had to get Sheriff Gough and then they were planning on coming to Pleasant Hill and cleaning this police department out here. He also said that in this blue Mercury these subjects had a gun in the car.

"He said that's all he remembered and he wanted to go

home. He didn't have any way to go home. I asked him if he would go home if I got him a taxi and he said that he would. So we called the taxi for him and gave the driver, Purvis Smith, ten dollars to take him to Holden."

My name is Purvis Smith. I am thirty-six years old. I work for the Pleasant Hill Taxi Cab Company.

"I got a call from the City Hall to take a passenger by the name of Pollard to Holden. I put the man in the car and took him to Holden and he talked all the way down there, telling me the different things he had done, and how many people he had killed. I told him—'I wouldn't do that if I was you.' And he said—'I'm going to come back up here and do some killing.' And I told him —'I wouldn't do that. You better go home and go to bed, you'll feel better in the morning.'

"But he said that wasn't going to satisfy him. He was going to get rid of the sheriff and the policeman that went off duty just before Simpson killed the policemen in Harrisonville and he was going to set Harrisonville on fire, he was going to set Pleasant Hill on fire, set Holden on fire. He said he knew he was liable to get killed, but he said—'I don't have forever to live.' He said he'd had a beard on his face and long hair but he noticed he was too conspicuous and he couldn't get around through the crowd and do his work, so he had his hair cut and his face shaved.

"I thought it was another one of them crackpots. I thought it was just dope and whiskey talking but at the same time I guess maybe that it wasn't."

THE Colonel watched it all, listened to the stories, pumped his gas, and was heartsick. The town was betraying him just like the Army had betrayed him . . . nobody was *man enough* anymore. There were Viet Cong on the courthouse steps, dope pushers at the roller rink, revolutionaries camouflaging themselves with haircuts so they could kill better . . . and the City Council and the Chamber of Commerce awarded themselves gimcracky plaques.

Retired Col. John A. Leach, forty-two, speaks with a honey-soft Southern drawl. He is tall, trim, and gentle; his face is lined and sagged; his eyes are the color of smoked glass and his hair is thinning and salt-and-peppered. He is calm, adamantine, and acts like a man used to the pressures of command. Angered, he doesn't bluster; he stares the man down, freezes him into compliance. In 1967 John Leach left the United States Army with two Bronze Stars, two Purple Hearts, and fourteen other medals. He was a veteran of World War II, Korea, and Vietnam.

He falsified his age to enlist and was drummed out when they uncovered his lie. He went back and was drummed out again, this time for splitting the lip of a pigdog major who was running a blackmarket wristwatch racket at a basic training camp. John Leach punched that major, knowing it would play hell with his career, because he believed in The Commandments and the United States Army. Shilling rabbit-hearted bootcamp kids was a gob of spit in the face of both the Creator and Uncle Sam. He loved the Army, tried to get back in, but couldn't.

He got as near the Army as he could. He went to a basic-training town in Arkansas and worked handyman jobs there, writing poetry (he never finished high school but reads voraciously) in his sparetime. He wound up doing janitor work in a courthouse and when the judge needed someone to index and move his law library, John Leach, lover of books, volunteered. The judge was amazed. His janitor asked to read some of the books at night, learned fast, and did a perfect job. They got to be friends and John Leach even showed the judge some of his poetry.

In seven days this piece of dirt called earth was made,
And shortly after this the foundation laid
For all the deceit, bitterness, selfishness and strife
That man has practiced for 100 million years of life.
And though it takes another hundred million to shake,
The house of steel that was made for man's sake,
There will never be another eden on earth for humanity,
For man has proven himself at nothing but stupidity.

The judge asked him what he was doing as a handyman, and John Leach told him he couldn't get back inside the United States Army because he couldn't countenance corruption. The judge had bigshot political ties; John Leach's Army file was stamped "VIP Influence" and Uncle Sam took him back.

This time he prospered. He read dozens of military books, studied till he couldn't keep his eyes open, and became a guerilla-war expert. He wrote a paper called "The Overlooked Aspect of Guerilla Warfare" and was awarded a superior commendation for his analysis of Mau-Mau terrorism. "Kenya is predominantly Negroid," John Leach wrote, "and the British were far superior in both weapons and organization. This superiority was not the deciding factor. The British controlled movement and screened all of the Negroids. The success here was primarily due to race. The British knew that *all blacks were suspect until proven otherwise.*"

He wrote another paper on the most effective way "to combat Communist tyranny." "It is the human beings on this earth that made the laws and it must be the human beings that enforce them. Do you ask a murderer to 'Please stop killing?' No, you try him and give him the supreme penalty as soon as possible to pay him for breaking the law and to set an example for others who might be inclined to do the same. There are no terms for a murderer, nor should there be for a nation who has aggressed against another for its own selfish gain. I don't claim we should plunge the jury of the world into a homicidal wave, but I do claim the aggressor should pay the supreme penalty. I think it would be for the betterment of the world to stop bartering with a butcher and teach him the meaning of right and wrong. The means of teaching would have to consist of something that would enter every man-atom of that nation and burn a scar on his soul and one that would also tend to be a lesson to any other nation with aggression on its mind. *What better means could we use than the hydrogen bomb?* It is possible to stop the aggression now taking place if we use the potential God has seen fit to place in our hands. *I further hold that the end justifies the means.*"

In 1965 John Leach, a member of the Inspector General's staff in Vietnam, was assigned to investigate PX corruption. He was appalled by what he found. "There were thousands of these big steel coffeemakers out in the middle of the jungle because somebody got a kickback. They'd buy the stuff, make their dirty dollars, and then cannibalize the coffeemakers with bulldozers." Corruption extended to the highest levels of the service and, working eighteen hours a day, John Leach ferreted a thick file of evidence. It implicated a Sergeant Major in charge of the PX program, working in cahoots with an officer a whisper away from the very top of the Vietnam command structure. He passed his evidence on to his superiors and waited for the courts-martial to begin. Nothing happened. "I realized after a while nothing was gonna happen, either, because some of those boys wearing an armful of stripes and medals were protecting each other." He quit the Army in 1967, betrayed and disillusioned. "I was Old Army. The New Army, I don't know where it comes from. I couldn't live with corrupation and follow orders given by men who were thieves and cheats."

He saw some news stories saying a Senate Committee headed by Senator Abraham Ribicoff, of Connecticut, was investigating the PX program, and went to Washington. "I paid for the trip. I went to the Army brass, still refusing to see the handwriting on the wall, and I said—'I've still got Xeroxes of some of my old files in case you didn't get them.' They couldn't run me out of Washington fast enough. They were afraid I'd go to *Roobicoff*. Well, I went to *Roobicoff* anyway. I dug out an old poem I wrote that said—'My body belongs to the Army but my soul belongs to God' and read it a few hundred times." He saw his country "rotted by a moral cancer" and he thought he knew the reasons: "The problem is affluence. We've lost sight of what the country stands for. Freedom isn't a right; you've got to earn it. Lying won't get you anywhere, whether it's the government that lies or the politicians."

John Leach, starting his life all over again, with a wife and three kids, looked around for a quiet place where he could settle, collect old books, "and have nothing in my craw." He chose Harrisonville. He'd saved up some money and used it to open a Gulf gas station outside town near the Interstate. He built a shed next to it where he sold guns and ammunition and gave tips on shooting trophy-age deer. It wasn't easy getting used to civilian life. "I'd never even voted all my life. I was in the military and, you know, you could discuss politics but not debate them. I was just an arm of the government. It didn't matter who was in office. I followed orders."

He liked the town and a lot of townspeople took a liking to John Leach. They knew about his medals and he always treated them friendly and fair. He was one of them; he never made them feel low and he cared about their problems. "I've been what you might call a common man all my life. I was a little kid when my parents separated and I worked a dozen jobs from the time I was thirteen. I know how tough life can be. My dad was in the Army, fighting a battle with the bottle. Well, when I got to Harrison-ville, the common folks around here saw I knew about those things."

He'd been in town about a year when "I got to learn about the power structure in this town. The square merchants and the councilmen, they like to lord it over the common folks. A lot of them are puffguts and boiled-shirts and fancy themselves real wondermen. They spend their time in the Harrisonville Hotel sipping coffee, gossiping, deciding the problems of the world among themselves. They have it easy. Nobody runs for council, that's part of the problem. Those people usually don't even get any opposition. The job doesn't pay hardly anything and most folks around here are too busy trying to make a living than to spend their time in a bunch of meetings.

"Then there are the fancy rich who are out at the country club all the time and at the Episcopal church pulling the strings. The mayor, Raine, is just a puppet for these people. He does what they tell him and he's able to have a few drinks whenever he

wants, get his picture in the newspaper, and act important. And
G.M. Allen, hell, G.M.'s just a shirt-tail who was a looey in the
War and never got over it.

"It's not such a clean town, either. There's the usual kind
of smalltown corruption. The rich folks always get out of their
little scrapes with the law. Big Cadillacs well known in town never
get ticketed, while some poor farmer who drives his pickup onto
the square, he'll get a ticket just as fast as the meter clicks off."

John Leach soon found that most of the people in his new
town were common folks who felt the same way he did and shared
his frustrations. They came to his gas station and spent their time
asking him questions—What did he think about the killings?
What could they do about the hippies? Was it going to happen
again? The Colonel became the poorman's proudly rednecked
champion, almost as distrustful of merchants as of longhairs. "I
had the feeling nothing was gonna be done and I felt a responsibility because I knew what this was about. I'd been in the service.
I knew about guerilla war and how to handle it. But I didn't know
exactly what I could do about it. I believe in God and the law and
I thought maybe I should run for office. But me? In politics?
Never even having voted?"

One summer day, walking through the clerk's office in the
courthouse, he saw a faded newsclip on the wall. It talked about
the time in the 1890's when the citizens of Gunn City stopped
a train, grabbed three officials who'd bilked them of their bonds,
and executed them by the tracks. Next to the newsclip was a sign
that said: "When Government Administration Breaks Down,
People Take the Law into Their Own Hands." When he got
outside, he glanced at the inscription on the courthouse that says:
"A Public Office Is a Public Trust."

The aldermen and those hotsy-totsy Chamber of Commerce

types weren't fulfilling the public trust; people were dead and the hippies sniggled at them in the noonday sun; the government administration was breaking down. The Colonel thought about it —"I don't like a no-win war. You don't fight a streetfight by Marquis of Queensbury rules"—went home, and looked up a word he didn't know much about: *vigilante.*

IT *was a xeroxed drawing, found one morning scotch-taped to the streetlights, parking meters, and trees around the square. One copy was thumbtacked to the courthouse door. There were two people in the drawing: a black man, caricatured with popout eyes and ballooning lips, and a white girl. The girl had long hair; her eyes were wide open; she was grinning. The black man had the words "WIN ALLEN" scrawled on his arm.*

They were both naked. The girl was bent over on all fours, palms and soles to the ground. She had muskmelon breasts and her butt, plump and ready for action, jutted high in the air. Pubic hair billowed from her loins. Her legs were spread wide apart. She was craning her neck at Win Allen, who stood behind her.

Win Allen was chained to an upside-down L-shaped beam. The chains were wrapped around his ankles and belly. His penis, a foot-long rattlesnake, hung limp to his knees. A string was attached to it. The string was hooked onto a pulley. At the end of the pulley, inches from Win Allen's black face, was a double-barreled shotgun. Another string was attached to its trigger. The gun was rigged to go off in Win Allen's face if his penis hardened and the string moved. In the space between the girl's spread-cheeked white ass and the barrels of the shotgun were the words: "THE SURE SOLUTION TO THE NEGRO PROBLEM."

. . . In the blazing summer of 1931, in Marysville, Missouri, a town not far from Harrisonville, Raymond Gunn, nigger, was

154 /

charged with violating and bludgeoning a kewpie-dollish twenty-three-year-old schoolteacher, Miss Velma Colter. Miss Velma was raped right in her schoolhouse, a few feet from her beloved old-fashioned piano. She died on the classroom floor, pretty blond head in her own blood. Gunn maintained he was innocent.

The night before the nigger's arraignment, a lot of folks stayed awake. Lights blinked in the farmhouses. Scrambled eggs and sausages were fried at dawn; a crowd collected around the courthouse, which stood in the middle of the town square, surrounded on four sides by choked streets and little shops.

Sixty-three-year-old Sheriff Harve England looked at the crowd and thought it looked calm. "I couldn't see any hostility in it," he said. At nine o'clock, he was in Judge D.D. Reeves's chamber. "I guess I'll go get him," the sheriff told the judge, "I guess it'll be safe." The sheriff took two deputies with him.

They walked a block to the jail and the sheriff told the nigger to get out of his cell. He fastened the nigger's wrists to an iron bracelet. A five-foot chain was attached to the bracelet. They got into the sheriff's new Packard. Townspeople stood on the sidewalks and watched. The sheriff stopped in front of the courthouse and one of the deputies got out first. The crowd surged.

"Stand back from here!" the deputy said. He drew his revolver.

The crowd leaped at him and took his gun away. They twisted the deputy's arms behind his back. The other deputy got out of the car. They grabbed at him. He resisted and was punched in the mouth.

"Niggerlover!" someone yelled.

"I don't care what you do with him," the deputy said, "but leave me alone."

The sheriff got out as if nothing had happened and tugged at the nigger's chain. Gunn got out and the sheriff pulled him through the crowd, asking people to make way. The crowd hemmed them in. The chain was torn from the sheriff's hands. The nigger was knocked down.

"Let the law run its course, boys," the sheriff said.

"We've got him! We've got him!" the mob yelled.

Upstairs, in the courthouse, some people rushed to the windows. Others ran downstairs with such force the courthouse door was knocked from its hinges. "I heard the commotion," the judge said, "I figured they were going to lynch him. I didn't even go to the window. I had cases to hear. I conducted the business of law."

A procession formed in the street. Heading it were the nigger and the leader of the mob, a tall dark man with a weathered face who wore a closely cropped mustache and a short reddish coat. The leader pulled the nigger by his chain. Another man pushed him, his hands under the back of Gunn's belt. Two others held him at the sides. "Hail! Hail! The Gang's All Here!" the crowd sang.

There were two thousand people in the mob. Women and children walked behind their men, honking cars brought up the rear. A Marysville policeman directed traffic. "I knew there would be a mess," the policeman said, "traffic was almost at a standstill."

The nigger was pelted with stones and clubbed with baseball bats. The clothes were torn off his sinful body. His testicles were pinched with motor pliers. Flesh hung from the iron bracelet on his wrists.

The procession headed for the schoolhouse where Miss Velma was raped and killed. There was a murmur when they got the nigger to the door. Blackboards were carried outside; windows taken from their frames and stacked in a neat pile. Miss Velma's old-fashioned piano was wheeled outside. Cans of gasoline and kerosene were placed on the floor. Boards were broken up in the center of the floor. A man walked in with a handful of kindling wood. The nigger begged for mercy.

"We're going to give you the same mercy," the leader said, "that you gave that girl."

The nigger was jerked to his feet and taken to the front of the room.

"This is where she was when you came in," the leader said. The nigger was made to kneel.

"This is where she ran," the leader said, pointing to the corner of the room. The nigger's face was pushed to the floor.

"Here is where she died," the leader said, "here's where we'll burn you."

Gunn wept hysterically. "Give me a chance," he said. "I didn't do it. Please don't burn me. I didn't do it."

"Spread the gasoline," the leader said.

The floor was soaked down.

"Burn him on top!" someone outside shouted. "Let's all see him!"

The leader ordered his men to construct a ladder. They found two pieces of lumber to serve as uprights. Other boards, half-rotten, served as the rungs. Rusty nails, yanked from the schoolhouse walls, were pounded into the wood with stone and bricks. The ladder was ready. It was placed at the side of the schoolhouse nearest the highway. Two men climbed up and took the shingles off the ridgepoles at the center of the building.

"Get him onstage!" someone shouted.

The nigger was brought outside. His head was bowed and his shoulders drooped. He was kicked in the groin and fell to the ground. When he got up, his shoulders straightened. He walked up the ladder steadily. One of the boards broke under him. He clutched at the ladder. He supported his weight with only his manacled arms. His bare bloody feet dangled in the air. He was pulled to the roof by his chain.

He stood there a moment, his skin glistening in the sun. "I didn't do it," he said. "You can't burn an innocent man." Three men forced him down on the roof, over the section where the shingles had been removed. He was half on one side of the apex and half on the other, facing the highway and the crowd. The chain fastened him to the pyre. It was tied around the ridgepole, passed over his body, and fastened to the exposed rafters. Men came out of the schoolhouse with the gasoline. They climbed up the ladder and handed it to the men on the roof. The nigger was drenched.

"Let her go!" the leader said. A torch was thrown inside the schoolhouse; another was thrown to the roof.

Smoke rose against the bright blue sky. Flames flicked at the windows and raced toward the nigger. A blast of fire passed across his face. He made no sound, but drew his head back. Another blast covered his arm. The nigger raised his arm in a fist and screamed. His body bulged against the chain. He screamed for more than a minute.

The rafters gave way and Raymond Gunn's body tumbled into the house of fire. An hour later the schoolhouse had burned to the ground. Men piled burning timber on the nigger's charred body.

No one was indicted; the sheriff said he couldn't recognize anyone; the governor said he had no authority. Souvenir-hunters stripped Miss Velma's piano naked . . .

THE Colonel who'd exposed an international Army scandal began investigating the shooting on his town square. "I knew the best way to get the truth was to go to the feedbox and get to the source," John Leach says. But the hippies on the square wouldn't tell him anything, so the Colonel went to what he considered the most reliable alternative. He talked to those teenagers who talked to the hippies.

As temperatures stayed in the 100s, John Leach discovered the "facts" of the shooting: Charlie Simpson was a hardcore drug dealer. He bailed his friends out of jail because he was panicked they'd squeal on his drug-peddling activities. "Two nights before the shooting," John Leach says, "the longhairs were drawing straws to see who'd pull the trigger."

They were getting ready to try to start their revolution again, John Leach said. His teenagers told him the hippies were stockpiling gunpowder. The Harrisonville Sporting Goods Store was burglarized and thirteen shotguns were stolen. One of the shotguns was found in the basement of one of the hardcore always up on the courthouse steps.

The Colonel unearthed the roots of the conspiracy: "I found out that one of the masterminds of their movement was a thirty-year-old female teacher in the high school. She told her class— 'America is a place where the rich get richer and the poor get poorer.' She taught them English and the first short story they read was about a young boy who goes up on a roof and sees an old woman sunbathing there. The old woman asks the boy to feel her up so she can teach him about the woman's body."

He shared his findings with his friends and customers and went to the square one day to see the revolutionaries with his own eyes. What he saw determined him to rally the town to action. "It was only a couple months after the shooting, remember. You might say the blood was still drying on the street. I watched them from the drugstore. One of the hardcore was sitting with a thir-teen-year-old girl, both hands under her blouse, holding her breasts. They pulled up an old green Chevy van. They took the chairs out and turned the radio up. A lady pulled into a parking spot and one of them stepped out and told her it was filled. There were no police around. The footpatrols weren't walking anymore. I think they were scared. None of the policemen wanted to get killed. In a way I couldn't blame them."

He thought about the young people he had watched: "I figured we either had to straighten 'em out or move 'em out. Some of them were beyond help, animals, just like mad-dogs. There's no cure for a mad-dog." And he thought: One of the first guys they should hang is Dr. Spock.

He felt he had a responsibility to the town, sat down at his typewriter, and pecked-out a letter to its citizens. He took the letter down to J.W. Brown at the *Democrat-Missourian* and said he wanted it printed. J.W. Brown read it and said he wasn't sure. The Colonel told him he'd pay for the space. If J.W. Brown didn't print it, "some of my boys will make copies and hand it out all over town." J.W. Brown called his friend, G.M. Allen, and asked him to read the letter. G.M. read it and said the Colonel was a "great patriot." The Colonel didn't have to pay for it; the Chamber of Commerce would foot the bill. The letter ran the length of four columns in the *Democrat-Missourian* and was set off from the rest of the page.

"I discovered Harrisonville in the spring of 1967," John Leach wrote, "After twelve moves in as many years, this seemed to be the ideal town to settle in my retirement. It had a small-town atmosphere where everyone was friendly and newcomers to the community were welcome. It had a good school system and a selection of businesses that would fulfill most needs. Young people gathered on the square and went to the drugstore for Cokes. The city law enforcement officers knew most of the young people by name and on many occasions advised and helped them.

"The 'Youth and Civic Center' was open and there was usually a dance on Friday or Saturday night. In the summer, the city swimming pool was usually full and the tennis court had its enthusiasts. The Drive-In Theater was a nice cool respite after a hot day in the sun. Oh, yes, Harrisonville had its share of problems that are common to small towns. The young boys would sneak a sixpack and occasionally get a ticket for speeding. Once in a while a school window would get broken, but all in all, it was an excellent place to raise a family.

"Times were good. The majority of the breadwinners had jobs. Wages were good. Even though a few in Harrisonville were on welfare, the vast majority were living good. The elders had their cocktail parties, golf course, bridge clubs, and a steady income. The young people got the family car and the fiver whenever they needed it. In many cases, they got their own car. Oh yes, a few worked and bought their own. They could run the streets and stay out late as long as their activities didn't interfere with the parents' social events. They were still good young people but without parental supervision or guidance.

"In many cases, the parents were completely oblivious of what, where, and when their children were doing or had done. Into this blase society moved a few hardcore extremists. No longer juveniles but adults. Young men and in some cases women who had been out in this world and met headon the realities of life and could not relate with them. Young people who turned inward on themselves and became parasites on society. To these parasites, our young people turned for a lack of concern by their elders. These were the "In" people. Man, they had seen the elephant, they knew where it was at. They promised new heights of delight, a way to beat the system. In addition, our news media played an important part in their development. These young people were bombarded with war, poverty, drugs, equal rights, and civil liberties.

"Now, for all the indifference of their parents, they had a cause, a direction and purpose. They were the children of tomorrow. Never mind that yesterday the elder generation were the children of tomorrow. Never mind that tomorrow they would be yesterday's children. Their problems (war, poverty, equal rights, civil liberties) were unique. What was WWII compared to Vietnam? What was the depression compared to the hungry child on the cover of LIFE? What was the race riots in the thirties and forties compared to Detroit? What was 'arrested and held for suspicion' compared to being 'busted' for possession of Mary Jane? Oh yes, their problems were unique—they had only been through it once while their elders had made the scene two or three times.

"But here on the Harrisonville square was where it was at, man! Here were elders who thought and acted as they did. Here were the cats with the answers. Here were the cats that thumbed their noses at society. They would provide the kicks, no longer derived from the drive-in, the teen dances, the Friday-night date. They would provide the guidance and leadership their parents had failed to give. Play Frisbee on the street, that's your right; never mind that you're blocking traffic and depriving others of their right of going about their business. Have a pine-cone fight around the town square; so what if you hit an old lady! Whoever heard of an old lady being killed with a pine-cone! Drive your cars around the square and park them three abreast; never mind that the people behind you are trying to get their child to a doctor. Park your 'pad on wheels' right beside the courthouse and turn your stereo to 200 decibels. Never mind that the county court is in session and the county clerk is trying to balance his books. Go ahead and take that pill; never mind the results of your actions. Go ahead and commit lewd or indecent acts at high noon on the courthouse lawn; never mind that young children as well as other people may be passing. You have as much right to these things as those old men who are there 'whittling and spitting.' Never mind that those old men worked forty or fifty years and earned their day in the sun. Never mind that they bother no one nor keep anyone from going about their business.

"So they hauled you in for indecent conduct? Didn't the judge find you 'not guilty' because there was no law against lewd acts on the courthouse lawn? Why should you work? Your old man has a job and it's his obligation to support you. You didn't ask to be born. So now, man, the word is out. Harrisonville is the place, man, anything goes!

"Society is what the majority make it and the small voice of Harrisonville isn't going to change that. The decisions of our higher courts have assured that the wrongdoer has as many rights, if not more, than the common man in the street. These courts go to great lengths to see that the rights of wrongdoers are upheld. So, in the long run, all our law enforcement officers can do is try to keep a semblance of order. That leaves us with the parents of young people in this town. Those 20- to 30-year-old 'cats' on the square are parasites. A parasite must feed on its host to survive. Eighty percent of the young people on the square are from Harrisonville. If these children, yours and mine, were well-behaved, supervised and disciplined, they would not follow. And, without followers, the parasites would fade away for greener pastures. They need these young of ours desperately to feed their egos and to get at us straights through our children.

"I believe in Harrisonville and its potential. I believe it is still a good place to raise a family. Let us assure the Mayor and City Council and anyone that might be interested that we, the majority, favor law and order!"

A note at the end of the Colonel's letter to the town said: "This letter so aptly sums up the situation in our community that we feel every citizen should have an opportunity to read it with serious consideration. Publication is sponsored by the Harrisonville Chamber of Commerce."

The letter, as John Leach says "stirred the town's feathers." It appeared only a few weeks before the Harrisonville Vigilance Committee, armed with shotguns and booze, occupied the square.

WHILE the Colonel sold his buckshot and waited, two outsiders—worse, eggheads—sat in a ritzy Kansas City suburb and made highfalutin plans to rescue the town of Harrisonville.

Dr. Jan Roosa is forty-five years old, stands well over six feet tall, and has Latin movie-star goodlooks. When he appears on a talkshow, he gets mash notes in his mail. He is Kansas City's most distinguished psychologist, the former president of the Greater Kansas City Psychological Association, cochairman of the Citizens Concerned for the Urban Crisis, and once a member of John F. Kennedy's White House Conference on Children and Youth. A Navy veteran born in Illinois, he is consultant to dozens of area schools and hospitals. He is a just-folks intellectual, down-to-earth, homespun, gifted with a quiet manner and lively sense of humor.

Dr. Gene Wagner is thirty-nine years old, stands a head shorter than Jan Roosa, and is owl-eyed and intense. He is an associate professor of economics and social science at the University of Missouri in Kansas City, a former Fulbright lecturer at the University of Guadalupe in Mexico. He specializes in the study of underdevloped areas. He is a committed and iconoclastic liberal: he led Kansas City's first anti-war protest in 1963, when he and seven others marched in the cold outside the Air Force Recruiting office. He is charmingly flamboyant, buoyed by a kind of highbrow flash. In style he is the complete antithesis of Jan Roosa, who is his best friend. "Ah, Jan," Gene Wagner will say, "when I'm fucked up, you're the only one who can give me hope."

Not long after the shooting, F. Russell Millin, chairman of the Missouri Law Enforcement Assistance Council, part of the federal government's LEAA program, visited Police Chief Davis and several aldermen in Harrisonville. Millin asked if Davis thought LEAA could ease the town's tensions. "The upshot of the meeting," Millin says, "was that they did request professional help to defuse an obviously explosive situation."

Millin turned to the men he thought ideal for the job, Drs. Roosa and Wagner, and asked if they were interested. Both men had read of the gunfire in Harrisonville; both felt the uniqueness of their backgrounds would help them save the town from further turmoil and bloodshed. They had a responsibility, they figured (John Leach had used the same logic) to help. They knew about communication and human dynamics (the way John Leach knew about guerilla warfare). Millin told Harrisonville officials the LEAA "Crisis Team" was on its way.

"We got into town at dusk," Gene Wagner says. "Our plan was to stay in the middle, to stay neutral, to learn about the place. We decided to talk to the kids first and arranged a meeting at a church hall. I didn't know quite what we were walking into. I mean, I've worked with some pretty heavy hardcore guys, like a Kansas City revolutionary who used to walk up and down the streets flipping pipe-bombs. Jan worked extensively with the Black Panthers. We were both active in the peace movement and cooled out a lot of guys who wanted to make war.

"We went up to the square and saw these guys dangling all over the place, told them who we were, what we were about, and asked them to come sit down and talk to us. We met Win Allen, Risner, the Thompson brothers, and they were friendly enough. They came over to the church."

The longhairs introduced themselves, shook hands, and said they didn't trust them. Maybe Roosa and Wagner were "spies" for the Necks. Someone said their credentials had to be double-checked with revolutionary Bros in Kansas City. "It was the passage rite game," Wagner says, "I had to demonstrate my intricate knowledge of the power-shake so many times that my hand hurt."

The final test was a bottle of Coca-Cola that Win Allen was drinking.

"Can I have a swig of that?" Gene Wagner asked.

"You wanna drink out of a bottle that a nigger was drinking from?" Win asked.

"Sure," said Wagner, "would you drink from a bottle a white man's drinking from?"

"No," said Win.

"Good," Wagner said, "that gives me the whole bottle."

"It was obvious," Wagner says, "that their radicalism was pretty unsophisticated stuff. You know, once I saw where they were coming from, it wasn't hard to lay on an even tougher radicalism trip. I talked a lot about the stupidity of the war. I used a lot of 'Right on's and I used 'man' every other word. One guy kept leaving the meeting, saying—'Hey, man, these guys are far out!' and more and more of their friends drifted in. After a while the whole room was filled.

"Win was the leader and after about an hour Jan and I pinned them down on the things they wanted, or the things they said they wanted. They said they wanted jobs without restrictions to hairstyles. They wanted the merchants to realize they weren't the cause of their money problems. They wanted the high school to teach more relevant courses; one of them said—'How can they say that Columbus discovered America when he was met on the beach by Indians?' They said the cops were threatening them and carrying riot guns and said one of the policemen had told them if they stayed on the square there'd be a shootout."

In the middle of the meeting, Jan Roosa took a telephone call. The call came from the two middle-aged sons of Orville Allen, the dry cleaner Charlie Simpson gunned down across the street from the sheriff's office. Allen's sons wanted to come to the church hall to talk to the hippies. Roosa tried to dissuade them but couldn't. "I thought," Wagner says, "good God! We've been here a couple hours and guns are going to be drawn. We're going to get a shootout at the OK Corral just as we arrive on the scene! The two Allen brothers walked into the meeting a few minutes later. I almost lost my cool. The situation was overwhelming."

"All we're here to do," one of the Allens said, "is find out why our father was killed."

Wagner says: "The two brothers were calm. It was obvious they were just two plain ordinary middle-class guys who loved their father and all of a sudden, for no reason they could see, he was shot down on the street. They couldn't comprehend it."

Win Allen took charge: "I can dig that," he told the brothers, "I can understand you're concerned."

Wagner says: "I knew then that our hardcore group was not made up of the toughs they were supposed to be. I'd been around gangs in New York who would have looked at those two pathetic guys and said —'Man, this is war, fuck off!' But Win was polite to them and said they were willing to talk. The time wasn't right, though, because they were meeting with us. The Allen brothers left as soon as they realized they could make contact.

"I knew too," Wagner says, "that these hippies were kids. I could communicate with them. Shit, these people were just like my students. This is how I make my bread. I make my living communicating with people like that."

Win Allen and his Bros agreed at the end of the meeting to discuss the problems of the town with City Council if Roosa and

Wagner could arrange it. The two eggheads analyzed their first contact with the town square desperadoes and decided: The longhairs were totally naive about the state of the Movement. They lacked commitment to any real political effort to bring about change. They lacked any political philosophy except for a "backwoods anarchism."

A few days later, Drs. Roosa and Wagner met with City Council. Wagner was confident: "I grew up in a small town outside New Haven, Connecticut. My old man was the mayor. I kept going back to his problems. He was kind of inspiring me to deal with these people. Our town had a big highway nearby and the highway brought my old man a lot of problems. I thought I could identify with the councilmen. I figured they were hardworking stiffs with power in the community, men with status as businessmen who'd earned the right to step to the front."

Before the meeting, he and Roosa discussed the aldermen. "I felt they'd be terribly concerned about what had happened," Wagner says, "they'd feel some degree of responsibility as civic leaders." Roosa told him: "Bullshit! These guys won't accept any guilt. They'll view the shooting as something that came down from the sky, caused by a bunch of dirty hippies, and they'll want us to help get rid of them."

The meeting began with formal introductions. Chief Davis and the city manager were also present. "When we went in," Wagner says, "we presented a contrasting mental image. Jan is so overwhelming, so tall, they immediately saw Jan as the leader."

Mayor Raine opened the meeting by fixing a fisheye on Gene Wagner.

"Are you sure you're not a member of the press?" the mayor asked him.

"No, sir," Wagner replied, "I'm an economist."

"Well," the mayor said, "we don't want any more newsmen

around here, they've done us enough harm."

"Then they started putting us through their test," Wagner says, "the same thing the hippies put us through, except now we had to prove how middle-class we were. I started using my old man, talking about his job as mayor, how hard he had it. I was calling him 'Daddy.' Well, never in my whole life did I call him 'Daddy.' Now it was 'my daddy this' and 'my daddy that.' I told them about how I grew up in that small town and how 'my daddy' worked with his hands for a while for thirty-five cents an hour."

"Shit!" the mayor said, interrupting Wagner, "you're a liar!"

"Now look here," Jan Roosa said, "we're not here to be insulted."

City manager Steven Berley, thirty years old, a man with heavy title and powderpuff influence, formerly the city administrator of Elgin, Ill., looked at Mayor Raine.

"Please," Berley said, "these people are here to help us."

Gene Wagner couldn't believe what he was seeing: Mayor Raine, purple-faced, his hands shaking, punched City Manager Berley. It was a stiff right hook, thrown in anger, that caught the city manager on his shoulderblades. He tried to duck the blow but couldn't swivel out of his chair fast enough.

"I told you to stay the hell out of our business!" the mayor said.

"I told you not to hit me," the city manager said, and slumped in the chair, staring at the table.

One of the councilmen stood up and started to say something.

"Sit down!" the mayor roared.

They somehow weathered the outburst and the meeting continued. "We've always done right by our youth," one of the aldermen said. "You can't do a goddamn thing because of the hippies," said another. "You can't even drive a car. You drive a car and the damn hippies tell you you're polluting the air."

"What we got on the square," the mayor said, "is a bunch of bums."

"We'd give 'em jobs," said alderman Felix Hacker, "if they'd only clean up."

"I wouldn't give any of them punks jobs," said one of his fellow aldermen, "they're just a bunch of lazy misfits."

"What do you think should be done?" Jan Roosa asked the City Council.

"They told us," Wagner says, "boy, did they tell us! They wanted the hippies off the square. They wanted them to stop making fun of them. They wanted them to stop harassing the merchants and stop talking about their revolution. They wanted them to stop talking to the high school kids and other young people. If they had a beef against something, they should talk to the mayor. The mayor said—'I'm an easy man to talk to.' They wanted them to develop some self-respect, which meant they had to cut their long hair."

Roosa asked the aldermen to meet with Win Allen and his Bros. They flatly refused. Roosa told them he wanted to form a Youth-Adult Community Council, and if the aldermen wouldn't meet with the longhairs, then maybe one of them could be a member of this group. They finally agreed. Felix Hacker, who was convinced the shooting was part of a hippie conspiracy, was the aldermen's delegate to the Youth-Adult Community Council.

"I sat there and watched them at their table," Wagner says, "and I still couldn't believe it. It looked like The Lord's Supper. The mayor was a genuine blowhard. All of them were afraid they'd be somehow scapegoated for what had happened. The whole meeting was some kind of surreal melodrama. There was even a councilman present who was almost totally deaf. He brought his taperecorder in, put it down on the table, and sat down. He didn't say anything all meeting. When the meeting was over, he picked the recorder up, took it home, and turned the volume all the way up so he could hear what was going on."

As the meeting ended, Gene Wagner noticed Police Chief Davis sitting behind him. "I remembered back home in Connecticut," Wagner says, "the police chief was a friend of mine. So looking at this poor guy who looked like Bucky Beaver, and looking at this rattlebrained council, I thought—How is this poor lunk supposed to keep order?"

"Gee," said Gene Wagner to Bill Davis, emphasizing the word, "this is really a helluva problem, isn't it?"

"Yeah, it's real tough," said the police chief, "I hope you're gonna help us."

"How do you mean?"

"Well, you're gonna be talking to the hippies and I hope you'll report anything subversive that you see. These people are Communists!"

"What do you mean?" Wagner asked.

"They read all this subversive literature."

"What literature?"

"The Red Manifesto, Abbie Hoffman, *The National Lampoon.*"

"Everybody reads that stuff," Wagner said.

"I don't read it," Davis said.

"I assign my students to read it."

"I figured you weren't going to help us," the police chief told him.

"I felt like grabbing all those guys," Gene Wagner says, "and saying—'Gentlemen, for God's sake, four men have died in the streets! Something has to be done!' I couldn't believe a community that close to Kansas City would have been so unaffected. I expected at least one or two of them to care; I didn't expect much."

The first meeting to discuss the Youth-Adult Community Council was set for the following week. Roosa and Wagner viewed it as the first tentative sign of any kind of progress. When they got to City Hall on the day of the meeting, alderman Felix Hacker was waiting for them. He was alone. None of the hippies had showed up.

"I was desperate," says Wagner. "That was it. The final straw. Nobody cared, nobody wanted to get involved. Why were we getting involved? I cooled down and Jan and I talked it over. I'd stall Hacker while Jan went to look for Win Allen. I started telling Felix fishing stories. I told him all the fishing stories I'd ever heard in Connecticut. I told him fishing stories I didn't even know I knew. I thanked God for my old man and all the fishing stories he'd bored me with through the years. Felix kept saying —'They're late, they probably won't even show.' "

Roosa says: "I got outside and all the hippies had mysteriously disappeared. The square was empty. I found where Win Allen lived and drove down there. I found him in the basement. 'Why aren't you at the meeting? I asked him. He played the dumb nigger. 'I forgot,' he said. I told him off and he admitted that he and Risner wanted to test us again—to see if we were really serious. I about took Win by the hand and we rounded the others up.

"I got to the bottom of the thing. They also didn't show because they didn't like the meeting being held in City Hall. That was 'Neck' turf and they were the 'Bros.' They wanted neutral turf, like a church hall. Well, they didn't know that Felix Hacker tried to line up some church halls but none of the churches would lend their space. Word of the meeting was out and some townspeople were so angry they were calling the councilmen Communists and niggerlovers for having one of their own sit down with the enemy."

Win Allen walked into City Hall with Jan Roosa, Rise

Risner, and some of their Bros, and Gene Wagner saw Win was in no mood to talk: "Win was uptight; his attitude was that this was class war. You get ten men and I'll get ten men and we'll have it out."

The purpose of the discussion was formation of the Youth-Adult Community Council. Felix Hacker had carefully prepared a list of businessmen he thought should be on the committee.

"Have you got a list?" he asked Win.

"I don't need one," Win said, "I know who I want."

"Well, what about some of the high school kids," Risner said, "maybe they should be on it, too."

The meeting adjourned only with the agreement there would be another meeting. Wagner told Felix Hacker he was going to talk to some of the high schoolers to interest them in the council. Felix smiled.

Wagner called the superintendent of schools.

"Can I come down and talk to the students and teachers?"

"I've heard about you," the superintendent said. "I'm not sure I want you talking to any of the students."

They agreed to meet for lunch at the Harrisonville Hotel. The entire school board was there. "It was a replay," Wagner says. "They said—'Why are you here? What's your interest? Why don't you go away?' I talked about my 'daddy' again. I told the same stories. It was a game. I was remembering things about my old man I hadn't remembered in years. They listened to me and they said—'We gotta get rid of the hippies! The leftwing element has taken over student council! They've turned our real good kids into revolutionaries!' I realized it would be impossible to get to the school."

Increasingly frustrated—"I kept running into *Catch-22*"—he tried another tack. Maybe the federal government could get jobs for some of the Bros, getting them off the square and easing tensions. Gene Wagner drove to Appleton City and talked to the regional director of the Office of Economic Opportunity. The trip took him a full day.

"What the guy told me was a horror story. The OEO had a branch office in Harrisonville but it was actually run out of town. To begin with, the City Council wouldn't give them office space. Then Chief Davis's police started ticketing their parked cars and the OEO people piled up huge parking bills. Then they got telephone threats. Then one of their men was threatened with a gun and told to get out of town. The director said the people hated poverty workers and government money as bad as they hated longhairs."

Wagner went back to Harrisonville and set up another meeting. "I know how pros work and I figured somewhere in that goddamn town there had to be a single pro." Jan Roosa was having doubts: "I was coming to the conclusion that the people who ran that town didn't want anyone more intelligent than themselves walking their streets."

Fifteen people attended the meeting. Win Allen was the only longhair present and he stole the show. He said he and his Bros continued to face harassment. He said he'd walked into a shop on the square and, after he left, the store-owner was told: "If you sell anything to that nigger, we'll burn you out!" He asked the merchant to file a complaint but the man said he was afraid. One of his Bros, Win said, had been roughed-up on the courthouse steps by two Necks.

Win Allen warned that if the townspeople didn't take action . . . if they didn't protect his Bros from violence . . . he'd "make war!" on Harrisonville.

The Nigger's "make war!" threat raced through town. Jan Roosa and Gene Wagner organized a few more meetings, one of them at the American Legion Hall, but nothing was accomplished. Wagner shepherded the shaky Youth-Adult Community Council, told the stories about his "daddy," and made the mistake once of quoting Mao Tse-tung. He knew it was deadly as soon as the quote was out of his mouth, the error of a bookreading man more accustomed to the campus than the Legion Hall.

A few days later, at the top of the page, the newspapers in Belton and Pleasant Hill ran letters to the editor which said Gene Wagner, "an outsider . . . was using Chairman Mao's sayings as a guideline to achieve the goals of the community."

"Whose goals?" the letters asked. "The goal of dissension? Revolution? Confusion? Class struggle? These are the goals to which Communism is rigidly dedicated. Any man who uses the Bible of Red Chinese Communism to guide his thinking while leading the deliberations of any meeting must identify himself with these goals. After the meeting, the professor held forth at length on the front steps of the Legion Hall on the follies and criminality of American involvement in Vietnam. In effect he ridiculed resistance to Communism on the American Legion's steps. He ridiculed the standards of Christian righteousness and conduct. In so doing, the professor has plainly stated where he will lead Harrisonville and thus, ultimately, Cass County. If for one moment you think we cannot become an exurban outpost of Communist confrontation, you have already fallen victim to the lullabye of coexistence.

"Our councilmen and influentials must be excused. In an emergency they accepted the professor's help, the first help that was offered. True to form, however, they dumped the problem in his lap and hastened back to the world of commerce. May I suggest that America, Cass County, Harrisonville, can solve their problems using Christians in concert without any help from the Butchers of Budapest and the Torturers of Tibet!"

Gene Wagner, outsider, left Harrisonville wornout and fedup. The egghead in concert with the Butchers of Budapest and the Torturers of Tibet! was flying back to his Connecticut birthplace. He wouldn't be telling stories about "my daddy this and my daddy that" for some time. He went home because . . . "my old man was dead, I had to bury him."

DAVID ROOSA'S DIARY

My name's Dave Roosa. I'm twenty-seven years old. My hair's long. Some people might think it's kind of freaky, but I don't. I've got a mustache and a beard and I'm married. I live on a farm north of Kansas City. I dig the land and farming and Jackie, my wife, who keeps me good company. I majored in sociology at the University of Missouri and graduated in 1968. I know about kids. I'm young and I'm turned on to a lot of things they're into. I love rock and I hate the war and I think we've got to change a lot of things in this country before it's going to be a really free country. When I was in school, I was the director of the Drug Education and Acid-Rescue Program, so you might say I know about dope. I also took a year's training with VISTA to work in Appalachia.

   I went down to Harrisonville because I could really get into it. I felt I could help and cool things out. I wasn't doing much at the time, anyway, just trying to get my head together. I was doing some construction work and daydreaming about going out to Colorado. I also went down there because my dad asked me to work on the Youth-Adult Community Council with him. I like to work on things like that. I believe that any two people can agree on some common ground. I used to believe that, anyway. I'm not that sure anymore. While I was down there, I kept a diary. I don't really know why I kept it. I'm not a writer. I thought maybe it might do some good sometime. Hell, I don't like explaining why I do things. As Popeye says: "I Yam What I Yam and That's All I Yam!"

May 30:

First evening on the square. Met Win Allen. He's got a lot of jive but makes it work for him. Digs his blackness and uses it to the best of his advantage. Also met two brothers, young, longhaired, part of the group on the square, Don and Terry Turner. Lots of young freaks hanging out or cruising the square waiting for something to happen. Nothing to do. Bored. Consensus of opinion: watch out for pigs and necks! No jobs, no one will hire or rent to freaks. The ones that I talked to—Win, Don, Terry—want things to change and get better, yet at the same time are talking non-involvement. On one hand they say they've all tried to work things out with the community without success, then turn around and say they don't need to work anything out, they just want to be left alone. They certainly like to drink wine and smoke dope. Dope rates about a C+.

Met the local police. Questioned as to why I was sitting in a car down the street from the police department. Suspicion was aroused because the car had Kansas City plates. They were nice about it. I was amused.

May 31:

Met Win on the square about five o'clock. Told him I got questioned by police and he said he expected as much. Again, young freaks hanging out, being bored, complaining about nothing to do. Met John Risner, Johnson and Jimson Thompson, and saw Terry Turner. We got into a car and started cruising. They wanted to party rather than talk and it seems to be one of their favorite solutions. Everybody misses Charlie Simpson. I was accused of being naive and not understanding how bad things really are in Harrisonville. John Risner seemed really surprised I was down there, but didn't have much faith in community coalition.

Sometimes it's hard to tell the freaks from the rednecks. Some of the rednecks are growing their hair pretty long. I heard several parents of young white girls are up in arms (literally) about their daughters hanging out with Win. Supposedly Win's life has been threatened by the father of one girl if he's seen with her again. He's digging on it.

June 6:

Arrived on the square around two o'clock. Found Win and immediately started talking about the trial of the night before. Win and some others were found guilty of disturbing the peace (a misdemeanor) but Win was found innocent of resisting arrest (a felony). Win got 60 days' probation and was fined $50 and court costs.

Win seemed really depressed, didn't know where he was going to get the money for either the fine or what he owes his lawyer. "I'm nothing but a poor dumb nigger that doesn't know anything and I keep getting fucked by the honkies." I started talking to Win about appealing the case. He said he didn't know about the rest of the group, but he didn't see how it would do any good. They continually get fucked by the town, the pigs, the courts, etc. No justice for them. Also, he said their group wasn't that 'together' anymore. The town has beaten them down so they can no longer take any direct action. Win went on to say that his group is scared of being shot, himself included, but his actions belie his words, for he continues to neck with white chicks on the square in front of everyone. This sends the town up the wall.

I spent most of the afternoon talking to Win about appealing his conviction and possibilities of what might happen in Harrisonville if they were willing to put out some positive energy. The more we talked about it the more excited he became. I also talked to him about the importance of taking part in the Youth-Adult Community Council meetings. He said he'd go for a while at least to see what the honkies had to say.

Win took me over to his house where he tried without success to convince his mother to get involved and come to the YACC meeting. Her reply was that she saw nothing to get involved in, it was a waste of time, and "they" didn't want her anyway.

Went to the meeting that night and was impressed by the thinking of a housewife, originally from Indiana, her husband from Harrisonville. Later her husband put pressure on her to drop out of YACC, saying she was neglecting her family.

June 7:

Got into the square around noon, and found Jimson Thompson. We talked for a couple hours about police harassment and the appeal. His contention is that the police let the Necks hassle the freaks and refuse to do anything about it. I suggested they file a formal complaint when they get hassled but Jimson said it wouldn't do any good. He went on to say some Necks pulled a knife on Win a couple nights ago and when Sgt. Jim Harris came by the square, Win told him about it and pointed out the ones who did it. Harris didn't do anything. I suggested they keep trying, one way being the appeal on the disturbance charge.

Jimson said it might work but he still didn't think it would do any good unless they make a "political" issue out of it. "We get hassled and thrown in jail by the pigs for something no one else would be busted for. Then we have to put up bail bond, then go to court where we're found guilty of a bogus charge, so we have to pay a fine, then we still have to pay a lawyer." He seems totally frustrated and unable to come up with any ideas of how to break the cycle. He feels that the only choice he's got is to either leave town or stay underground. I asked him why he wasn't around the square more often and he said he hides out during the day.

Sat around with Win and bullshitted with the young freaks on the square. Everybody's going to Arkansas soon—soon as they can get it together—soon as they get some dust—soon as they can buy some land down there—Soon. We talked about an ecology program in Harrisonville. I suggested we pick up all the trash on the square, even convinced a few others to join in.

Jimson Thompson came by again and he said he didn't think the appeal was going to accomplish anything. "That would only cope with the problem, not solve it." When I suggested he was copping out, he said "wait til the revolution and I'll be up on the square with a gun and may the best man win." Risner was in agreement——"fart it off."

Went out to the Turner farm with Gary Hale, Don Turner, Win Allen, George Russell. I told them to appeal their cases— beat the system at its own game, show the people they were unwilling to accept themselves guilty. Few of them saw any hope nor were they willing to commit themselves. It had to be all or nothing. They were unwilling to accept anything less than changing the whole world. They see themselves as the only ones who have a stake in fighting pollution, war, injustice, discrimination, etc. (Win doesn't do nearly as much talking when some of these older guys are around.)

I was also astounded by the extreme double standard that came out. Girls are seen as objects of pleasure, money, or service, and not much else, and they are treated accordingly. Furthermore, most of the males in the older group are from 20 to 28 years of age, while the girls range from 14 to 18. It's my feeling that these guys couldn't handle anything more sophisticated than a 16-year-old chick.

June 8:

Attended the nightly party. Around 7:30 the action picks up around the square. People are off work, have had dinner, and it seems that everybody in Harrisonville cruises the square. It's been really hot. After driving around for a while, everybody decided to go swimming at the city lake. Gary Hale, Risner, George Russell, some of the others were there. As the night progressed, many of the younger crowd arrived.

It's against the law to swim in the lake, although the group all said the water was polluted and the city no longer used this particular lake for drinking water. I was warned that we might be busted by the "pigs." Yet the whole evening they couldn't refrain from yelling obscenities and defiance across the lake at fishermen, picnickers, etc. We still could have been arrested, but it would have been a lot cooler if they had been quiet and peaceful.

The discussion began to center around the problems of Harrisonville in terms of "levels of consciousness." Risner believes the Necks haven't reached as high a mental state as he and are therefore inferior to him. At one point in the evening, Risner complained about what the Germans did to the Jews (Germans = Necks, Jews= freaks,) then later that night suggested that all the straights who are "fucking" this world should be put behind bars and should be "gassed." I tried to point out to him that he was saying exactly the same thing that he was putting "them" down for. He just wouldn't see it. I also think he was pretty drunk by this time. I suggested that they try being "easy" with the people in town. Just be and let the people of Harrisonville feel them out instead of pushing the group's "rights" and "freedoms" in their faces. That they really try communicating. The responses I got were: "I'm on such a high level I couldn't even come down that low again . . . it wouldn't work here . . . they've got to change first."

One of the group's favorite activities is getting "loose," which for a lot of them seems to be getting as drunk and stoned as possible, then talking about what a raw deal they're getting from society. Lots of escapism.

The freaks have turned Charlie Simpson into some sort of folk-hero-martyr for their cause. Also, members of the group are unwilling to criticize another member of the group, regardless of their actions and behavior, for fear of being criticized themselves. As long as you're a member of the group, whatever kinds of behavior you wish to engage in is fine—you're just "doing your own thing."

Jimson Thompson named his horse "Ootney."

June 11:

Obscene flyers threatening Win were found tacked around the square. Win seems more pleased than upset. He's got to learn to keep his hands off white chicks when he's on the square in front of the town.

June 12:

Gary Hale, his brother, Steve, and Harry Miller filed for appeal on the disturbance charge, with the help of a young ACLU lawyer from Kansas City. Win claimed he didn't know he needed the money today, that he didn't have it anyhow because none of the honkies would give him a job, so he'd have to borrow the money from his friends. He'd have it tomorrow. He pulled his "poor dumb nigger" routine.

Although only three people were filing, a group of about ten kids accompanied them to the police station. About the time we started walking toward the station, Don Foster came out of his Sears store and followed us on the other side of the street. I'd have to say the police were shook yet they didn't seem particularly hostile. They definitely were not ready for the appeals. Sgt. Jim Harris couldn't find the right forms, and neither he nor the municipal clerk knew what to do. The judge was out of town. It took all afternoon to file the appeals. Practically the whole time the freaks hung out in the offices and halls of the police station, causing anyone who came in or went out to step over or around them They also insisted on making negative comments on having to be there. All in all, the police were very cool. Upon leaving, Win said he hated being hassled by the pigs. I tried to point out we hadn't been hassled at all, but he replied that anytime he had to deal with the pigs he was being hassled.

June 13:

Win decided to back out. He said he couldn't get the money for the appeal bond, although it became obvious that he hadn't even tried. Even if he did appeal, he said, it wouldn't do any good, it was just playing their game. He says he's going to skip town—not pay his disturbance fine, just split, "slide on out." "I'm tired of their game and they'd be happy if I left town, that's what they want."

June 14:

I met Charlie Simpson's father in Harrisonville. He had come to collect the bond money which Charlie had posted the morning of the shooting. He's tall and thin, walks with a cane, stands erect. All the hippies pay him a great deal of respect, opening doors for him, getting him cokes, coffee. At the same time, Mr. Simpson expresses sympathetic feelings for them, especially those who were close to Charlie. He says what his son did was bad, but the town should leave the kids alone.

Win asked Mr. Simpson if he could borrow $50 for his appeal bond. Without hesitation, Mr. Simpson gave him the money. "You're a good boy, Win, you all are, I know you'll pay it back."

That's kind of funny. Charlie Simpson paid Win's bond for the disturbance charge and now Charlie's father was lending Win the money to make his appeal.

June 15:

I've been trying to persuade the freaks to find some other place to hang out, rather than hanging around the square, on streetcorners, in front of stores. They block the sidewalks and doorways so it's necessary for people to walk around them. They insist on flaunting their flagrant visibility in the town's face. The town is tight. To the suggestion that they try hanging out in the park outside town, the usual replies were: 'No one else is down there . . . Why should we, this is a public sidewalk and we have a right to be here . . . nothing's happening at the park . . . they'd try to run us out of there, too."

I've tried to explain to them how their continued presence

on the square has negative results on the Youth-Adult Community Council, but they place the blame on the townspeople. For all of his lip service about wanting to help, Win Allen, because of his behavior around the square and his negative influence over the younger freaks, is possibly one of the greatest deterrents to communication.

I tried again to talk to Win about the need to be more discreet in his affairs with white chicks, but he wouldn't hear of it. He's got the same rights as everyone else, except he's black. Besides, he says, it blows their minds. He either doesn't realize that his life might really be in danger or he doesn't care.

It's really hot. Each day seems to get hotter. The sun looks bigger and bigger in the sky, closer and closer, right on top of us.

JOHN Leach's oldest son, Bob, was home on leave from Vietnam. The Colonel walked the streets proudly with his boy, who wore his uniform and talked about slogging through the ricepaddies hunting VC. Thursday night, the 15th of June, Bob Leach drove around town with one of his buddies, Phil Young. Known as the roughest man in town, Phil Young is twenty-eight years old, stands 6 foot 6, and weighs 275 pounds.

The two drove to the square to look at the hippies Bob Leach was hearing so much about and to retrace Charlie Simpson's path. Phil pointed to the spot where the patrolmen were killed and they drove by the Retirement Home wall where the mad-dog bit his final bullet.

George Russell was sitting on the courthouse steps in his frayed bluejeans and Army fatigue jacket chopped off at the shoulders. He wore nothing underneath it but the pimples on his chest.

Phil Young says George Russell called them pigs and asked Bob Leach why he wasn't in Vietnam bayoneting babies. George Russell says he was minding his own business when Phil Young yelled: "Why don't you get a haircut, hippie?" George Russell says he got angry, put his hand to his groin, and replied: "Come here! I got something for you!"

Phil Young punched George Russell in the mouth, shattering teeth, and in the nose, drawing a torrent of blood, and then in the eye. People came running and heard George Russell say: "Goddamn you! Come back with your Neck friends tomorrow and we'll see who controls the square!" Like Win Allen's "make war" threat, George Russell's challenge wildfired through town.

Friday, the 16th of June, was doghot. Temperatures stayed in the high 80's all Thursday night, the humidity was soaring, sleeping was tough. Late Friday afternoon, the pickup trucks started blocking traffic on the square. By 7:30 that night, there were more than 150 men there. John Leach says the gathering was spontaneous: "Everybody just drifted up there after what the hippie said." Once John Leach got on the square, though, he admits he assumed command. He says he took charge because what he saw was enough to scare the shit out of any Bible-reading man: "There were two reasons for us being up there: to scare the hippies out of town and to wake the town up. We didn't want to kill anybody, at least I didn't want anybody killed. But when I got up there, I saw shotguns all over the place. Just about every pickup had a shotgun in it and there were some boys who were playing with them on the courthouse grass. I saw one boy racing around the square driving with one hand and sticking a hoglegged revolver out the window with the other."

The men split into four groups to more effectively patrol all sides of the square. A reporter from the *Kansas City Star* showed up, started asking questions, and was cursed. "If you got any brains at all," he was told, "you're not gonna stay around here." The reporter dutifully called his city editor and left. A group of longhaired high school Teeny-Bros drove by. Their car was stopped. "Get your asses out of town!" one of the men told them. The driver giggled and said: "Shit, we've got a right to be here." The kid was taken out of the car, slapped until tears and snot dribbled down his face, and placed behind the wheel. He drove away. The men cheered. "God Bless America," someone sang.

take him for a ride in the woods. They had it all mapped out, who was going to do what. They already had the farm picked out where they'd cut him. They'd collected their knives together, they'd already sharpened up these big Arkansas toothpicks. Well, I searched out the boys who were gonna do the cutting and I tried to talk sense to them. It wasn't easy. They wanted to cut the boy real bad and hang onto their souvenir. I finally got through to them but I wasn't absolutely sure. I said—'If you cut the Nigger you're gonna have a hundred federal men in here.'

"But I wasn't sure whether I could keep a handle on [...] thing, so I formed a squad of four boys I knew I c[...] Young was one of them. They were supp[...] of the vigilantes to make sure nob[...]

Saturday night, the vig[...] walked the courthouse in shift[...] kids drove through again and w[...] the car window down and a vigila[...] him. The car speeded away. The v[...] and photographer for the *Kansas Cit[...]* to get out of town if they wanted to s[...] trucks followed them to the Interstate[...]

At the far end of Pearl Street, a lo[...] to meeting his friends Saturday nights, wa[...] Some of the vigilantes spotted him. The[...] wasn't fast enough. They threw him to the[...] concrete, and someone said: "Get a knife!" thing!" the kid screamed. While he struggled a[...] knelt on his back and chopped his hair off with a [...] kid ran down the street, holding his head and sc[...] hysterical parrot. They tied his hair with a rubb[...] potvaliantly draped it like a flag on a shotgun.

"There was a lot of talk Saturday night about th[...]

Harry Miller's parents drove through the square on their way home. "That's that hippie's father!" someone yelled. The car was stopped with a shotgun. "Get out and stay out!" The Millers fled. "The boys up there," John Leach says, "why I knew them all. They were the working people of the town. Some of them might call them rednecks, but they're my friends. Some of them had longer hair, too, not hippie hair, but mod hair. They were tired of what was going on. They behaved like they were people. Cases of beer and bottles were passed around and I at a picnic. Some of them got a little likkered up. It was a think some of those boys were a Fourth of July picnic. One boy hot-diggity-dog kind of time. Some of them get up and made said—'This is it! We're not gonna let 'em get to be, you know, girls! They're not gonna insult our wives!' " at a picnic. We're not gonna let it get any more of our speeches just like you'd hear hippies and see that

"I tried to take control and not let it hot-diggity-dog kind of bloody. I got up and told them—'Boys, what we've got to do is make our points. We either have to scare the hippies out of town or into shaping up and we've got to let 'em know if they won't Council, we'll do it!' I told 'em, too, to look around and see that uphold it, we'll do it!' I told 'em, too, to let 'em know if they won't there were no merchants up there with us. So one of the boys got chants up and started yelling—'Where are the merchants? Get the mer-

Neither police nor sheriff's deputies took any action. They drove around the square and waved good-naturedly at the men. Sheriff Bill Gough walked around and chatted with his constitu- ents. "We stayed up there most of the night," Leach says, "drink- ing, talking about our problems and then everybody went home to sleep it off. We agreed we'd have a meeting in the afternoon and come back Saturday night."

At the meeting Saturday afternoon the men decided to call

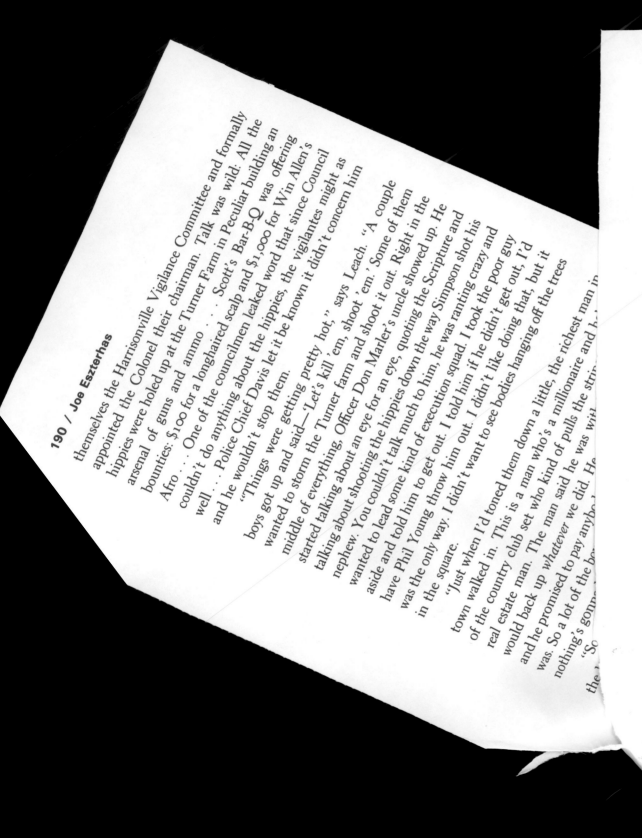

themselves the Harrisonville Vigilance Committee and formally appointed the Colonel their chairman. Talk was wild. All the hippies were holed up at the Turner Farm in Peculiar building an arsenal of guns and ammo . . . Scott's Bar-B-Q was offering bounties: $100 for a longhaired scalp and $1,000 for Win Allen's Afro . . . One of the councilmen leaked word that since Council couldn't do anything about the hippies, the vigilantes might as well . . . Police Chief Davis let it be known it didn't concern him and he wouldn't stop them.

"Things were getting pretty hot," says Leach. "A couple boys got up and said—'Let's kill 'em, shoot 'em.' Some of them wanted to storm the Turner farm and shoot it out. Right in the middle of everything, Officer Don Marler's uncle showed up. He started talking about shooting the hippies down the way Simpson shot his nephew. You couldn't talk much to him, he was ranting crazy and wanted to lead some kind of execution squad. I took the poor guy aside and told him to get out. I told him if he didn't get out, I'd have Phil Young throw him out. I didn't like doing that, but it was the only way. I didn't want to see bodies hanging off the trees in the square.

"Just when I'd toned them down a little, the richest man in town walked in. This is a man who's a millionaire and h... of the country club set who kind of pulls the str... real estate man. The man said he was wil... would back up whatever we did. He... and he promised to pay anybo... was. So a lot of the b... nothing's gonn...

"So...

the...

Leach says. "We all knew the real facts by then, how the hippies planned it and drew straws. A lot of the boys started talking about the prosecutor and the merchants and why they still weren't there. 'All they want is our money,' one of the boys said. Everybody had a lot of beer and whiskey by then and so everybody went home. We said we'd come back Sunday."

Sunday afternoon, John Leach pumped his gas. So many new customers pulled in he was afraid he'd run out. A middle-aged man in dark green workclothes came in and said—'I was up on the square and there ain't a hippie in sight.' The Colonel grinned and accepted the man's compliment. Another man told him—'I wanna congratulate you, Colonel. It's about time somebody did something around here."

A reporter from the *Kansas City Star* interviewed him and Leach said: "We realize this isn't exactly the American way of doing things. But it was the last resort. We'd tried everything and nothing else worked." The reporter went to see Police Chief Davis and told him about his colleagues who'd been chased out of town. The chief smiled. "Yeah, I heard about that," he said. The reporter asked him about the kids who were beaten up. "Oh," the chief said, "some of 'em may have got kicked."

Sunday night Win Allen made the mistake of wanting to see the vigilantes for himself. He thought he'd sneak into town and peer at them from an alley. One of the vigilantes saw him and yelled: 'The Nigger! There's the Nigger!' Win Allen ran for his life, with thirty vigilantes in pursuit. He outran all but one. The vigilante, inches behind him, tried to grab Win Allen by his kinky black hair. He sprawled to the ground, Win Allen's frizzy Jimi Hendrix Afro wig in his hands. Win got away. The Nigger's wig was paraded to the square. "Let's burn it," someone said. "Naw," said another vigilante, "let's keep it for a souvenir." The souvenir-hunter won.

"I thought I had the whole thing pretty well cooled by then," John Leach says. "Sunday night we decided we were gonna take the square one more time, on Monday. This time we wanted all the merchants there, the councilmen. We wanted some answers." The vigilantes gathered Monday and chanted: "We want the merchants! We want the merchants!" The merchants left their shops and walked somewhat shakily to the courthouse. "I wasn't exactly sure about going over there," says Felix Hacker, "but there was nothing else to do. They were raising more hell than the hippies did."

"We're tired of all this bullshit," one of the vigilantes told them, "if you people don't make sure there's law, we'll do it."

John Leach interrupted: "No matter who's up here, whether it's the longhairs or us, it's bad for business."

A town meeting was hastily called. The courthouse doors were opened and vigilantes, merchants, and aldermen trooped inside. The vigilantes shouted their demands: ". . . What are you gonna do about the hippies camping up here and about the hardcore? What about a curfew? What about investigating the killings? What are you gonna do to stop drugs?"

They presented a list of "concerns" compiled by John Leach: "Problems of juveniles and how they can be handled . . . Possibility of curfews as a method of control . . . Who has control over courthouse and yard, streets and sidewalks?. . . Who calls a grand jury investigation?. . . Drugs—why hasn't any evidence been uncovered? Why hasn't some action been taken?. . . How do state patrol, police, and sheriff work together?. . . What can a private citizen do to show some support for proper and necessary policing activity?. . . Can volunteers be deputized as auxiliary police?"

The merchants and aldermen praised the vigilantes' "patriotism and concern" and promised fast action. "You don't have to worry," one alderman said, "we'll do something fast."

The vigilantes went home and the next day, a kneehigh sign stood on the courthouse lawn that said: "Keep off the grass and wall—by order of the County Court!"

The very next week, City Council passed a new curfew which threatened jail terms for both juveniles and parents. "Loitering" on the public streets after eleven o'clock was punishable by a maximum penalty of $500 and three months in jail for both violators and their parents. Mayor Raine promised new efforts to reopen the investigation into the killings. G.M. Allen promised to "upgrade" the Chamber of Commerce Drug Abuse Committee.

John Leach's boy went back to Vietnam and the Colonel was trying to decide whether he should run for mayor—"Raine is the most profane man I've ever met"—or go to the Calvary Bible School to become a minister—"The Lord is of vengeance: he smote the Philistines."

George Russell filed charges against Phil Young for smashing his teeth and giving him a black eye. A hearing was set, but George Russell didn't bother to go; the charges were dismissed.

DAVID ROOSA'S DIARY

June 19:

Harrisonville blew up again over the weekend. Went to the Turner farm around 5 P.M. There were guns all over the place, including two stolen shotguns. Most of the older freaks had been there all weekend. They'd armed themselves and holed up. They stayed drunk all weekend, going into town only to purchase more liquor, then back to the farm. Sometime during this period three shotguns were stolen from a store in Belton and hidden at the Turners.

Mrs. Turner was practically hysterical with fright, afraid the vigilantes were going to kill her boys, and wanting to know what gave the vigilantes the right to do something like that. Mr. Turner, on the other hand, maintained as he has all along that all the hippies have to do is get haircuts, that would solve all the problems. He also stated that if there were to be any haircuts given in his family, he'd do the cutting and if any of the vigilantes set foot on his property, he'd shoot them. I see now why they call him Archie Bunker.

Drove into town with Don and Terry in hopes we could find some of the others and drive to the Turners to talk about the situation. As we drove into the street leading to the square, a redneck drove his truck into the intersection trying to block our way. He got out and started yelling at us that we'd been warned to stay out of town and if we didn't, we knew what would happen to us. I just drove around him on through the square. The vigilante group had not yet started to collect.

We found George Russell and Gary Hale and Steve Hale and drove back to the Turners'. Although they talked a great deal about a shootout with the vigilantes, it was obvious that was not what they wanted. For all their militancy, the freaks were scared and didn't really want a showdown. George Russell said he couldn't fight it any longer and he was leaving for Oklahoma to live with relatives and find a job. Win had already left town after being chased by a group of vigilantes. John Risner had tried to call Attorney General Kleindienst in Washington over the weekend. Risner was drunk and when he couldn't get him, Risner began to rant and rave and then hung up.

One of the things they were most upset about was that they saw the police as doing nothing the whole weekend. This was another example for them that the police were not interested in law enforcement, but were part of a conspiracy to run the old group of freaks out of town. "If we'd been up on the square drinking and had guns, they'd arrest us in a minute." I told them I didn't have any answers. The whole weekend was given to me as just another example of why they couldn't work within the System.

June 20:

Met Don and Terry Turner after they got off work and went with them to the Turner farm in hopes of convincing them to participate in the Youth-Adult Community Council. Terry is extremely hostile to any idea that all the various groups in Harrisonville can get together, find common ground, and talk out problems. His solution is total non-involvement, until something affects him personally and then respond to the situation in kind, i.e., an eye for an eye. He went on to say he wouldn't go out of his way to cause trouble, but if the rednecks or vigilantes ever beat him up or cut his hair, they'd better do a good job of it, because as soon as he was able, he'd kill them. I tried to point out that violence was never a lasting solution. His response was that he didn't care, they got what they deserved. He finally said that he had his beliefs and I had mine and I wasn't going to change his mind at all, so I might as well not try. I didn't feel there was much more I could say, so I changed the subject. I did suggest he remove the stolen shotguns from his parents' house.

Don's easier to talk to in that at least he's willing to try to see other points of view and alternatives. He seems to realize that the situation can only get worse the way things are going, yet can't quite commit himself to the involvement of trying. Says that he'd like to help, but doesn't see much hope for improvement. Says that you can't talk to the rednecks, they won't be satisfied until all the freaks have been run out of town. He's afraid that his involvement may make him less acceptable to his peers. Talks at great length about buying land in Arkansas and moving there. Land in Arkansas seems to be the ideal change for most of the them.

June 21:

The Youth-Adult Community Council meeting. The meeting was well-attended, mostly because of the confrontation over the past weekend. The vigilantes showed up, a faction that had never been there before. John Leach was their spokesman. Most of the meeting was spent in discussion of the past weekend, with charges and countercharges. There was a great deal of hostility and the discussion was extremely heated with many people willing to place the blame on anyone except themselves. During the meeting many of the young people got up and left. The discussions were generally monopolized by a few, usually adults, with the youths either unwilling or afraid to enter the discussions.

June 22:

Went to see Don Turner at his construction job and chewed his ass for not showing up at the YACC meeting. He said that he'd decided nothing would be accomplished by his presence, and I told him that nothing was going to be accomplished without it.

In the words of Eldridge Cleaver, he was either part of the problem or part of the solution, and as long as he and the rest of the group remained uninvolved, they were part of the problem. My feeling was that most of his reluctance was either peer-pressure or his own fear of having to produce.

June 23:

The high school kids that I met seem to be the most positive group to work with. They are eager and seem more than willing to work for what they want if they see any chance for its accomplishment. They're much more positive than the street-people. But they too are being turned off and turned away by the local Establishment, especially the school system. They tell me school spirit is at an all time low. Students don't feel that the school gives them options to do anything that would instill school spirit. Students are interested in other things. "Our worlds are larger now. We talk about national elections instead of proms."

June 26:

Win Allen is back in town. He only made it as far as St. Louis. When asked why he came back, he said that Harrisonville is his home. He didn't like St. Louis, but, most important, he said, was that the blacks he met in St. Louis were trying to pretend they were white. "They all walk around trying to be honkies." When asked about his own black consciousness, he said he didn't have any black pride, but just pride in being a human being, human-pride. He went on to say it didn't matter to him what color he was—he was just one human being relating to other humans, but the people of Harrisonville won't let him forget he's black. That's why he sees it as his right to mess around with white girls, two human beings relating, and if he should get shot because of it, it's because the honkies haven't attained his level of consciousness.

Still an extreme amount of hostility and several of the street people are talking revolution and having it out with the rednecks. Regardless of how much I try to reason with them, the only solution they can see is more violence.

June 27:

Spent most of the afternoon trying to get youth involved and willing to participate in YACC. Absolutely no attention span on the part of most of them. The rest don't know how to get involved, or are afraid. Win can't keep his mind on anything but making it with chicks, and his own ego trips, so that the only thing he puts out is a bunch of bullshit to cloud the issue. The rest are so self-righteous they can't see how their own behavior affects what happens to them. Soon as they get bored or are in disagreement with what someone says, they get up and stomp out.

June 28:

Met with a small group in the City Park to discuss ways of communication with the town. Win continually confused ideas and issues and threw up smokescreens by refusing to deal with a single situation. Whenever he began to find himself pinned down, he always reverted to talking about his rights and all "they" had to do was leave him alone. He effectively monopolizes the conversation, thereby controlling most of the session. Win always tries to talk "intelligent" to impress the younger group.

June 29:

Talked with Win. He's dropping out again. Says he's given YACC and the people of this community every opportunity to prove they're not racists and white supremacists. He's been bad-mouthing the organization all day to the younger street-freaks. He carries enough weight that he can pretty well pull that group any way he goes. That's a group I've been trying to work with particularly since I've been down here, but I haven't found any way of breaking Win's influence over them and he has consistently stood in the way. He left the last meeting shortly after it started to go home and watch a rock special on TV.

July 1:

I talked with a group of the hippies. Since they can no longer congregate on the town square proper, they now gather on a street corner across from it. The problems of the square have moved fifty feet. The rhetoric hasn't changed at all.

I'm really beginning to dislike hippies. Generally the talk centers around their wants, their rights, what's wrong with the town, and what a bum rap they're getting. Talking to them about the need for planning and organization is like talking to the blank wall. They either can't grasp it or they don't want to put forth the effort. And for all the lip service they pay to the ideals of peace, brotherhood, and a better world, they can't see the unreality of it because of their non-involvement. They are so sure that only they have *the* right answer (to everything.) In many ways they are much more conservative than many of the adult members of the community.

THE two outsiders, Drs. Roosa and Wagner, learned they were philanthropists. The Missouri Law Enforcement Assistance Council wasn't going to pay them for the time and money spent in Harrisonville.

The man who'd asked them to go to Harrisonville, F. Russell Millin, resigned as the council's chairman. Bill Smith, the executive director who'd given him permission to start the project, now said he hadn't approved it after all. So F. Russell Millin wrote a letter to Jerris Leonard, head of the Law Enforcement Assistance Administration in Washington that said: "The principle involved, the injustice that has resulted, and the matter of LEAA commitments are of extreme importance." Jerris Leonard took no action; Drs. Roosa and Wagner made plans to sue the LEAA.

Their application for a separate $52,000 grant to aid the people of Harrisonville was turned down. William Culver, executive director of the Missouri Law Enforcement Assistance Council, said he was refusing it because Mayor Raine and the council weren't in favor. Mayor Raine said he wasn't in favor because Mr. Culver had refused it. So F. Russell Millin wrote another letter, to the new chairman of the Missouri Law Enforcement Assistance Council. "In essence," wrote the former chairman to the man who'd succeeded him, "we have Mr. Culver on the one hand saying he rejects the application because the City of Harrisonville doesn't want it, and on the other hand we have the City of

Harrisonville rejecting it because Mr. Culver has rejected it. In my opinion, the whole program has been halted by Mr. Culver and Mayor Raine." The new chairman took no action; Drs. Roosa and Wagner gave up. It all went down the tube, even the deal they'd worked out with the Kansas City Police Department. Two Kansas City cops were to be assigned to work fulltime in Harrisonville so two Harrisonville cops could take advanced police and community relations training. Police Chief Davis fixed that. "We don't need more training," he said.

Dave Roosa stayed in town and worked with the kids he could reach. The Youth-Adult Community Council, which Drs. Roosa and Wagner had organized, remained the only link between the generations. Dave Roosa "worked like hell" to keep John Leach's interest alive and "farted off" Win Allen, Rise Risner, and their Bros.

YACC organized two events. A "Thank You Day" was held "to show appreciation to the adults for their efforts, progress, and facilities made available through the years." "I almost gagged," says Dave Roosa, "but at least people were talking to each other." The Up With People singers performed, and so did the Barbershop Quartet. A greased pole contest was the highlight.

Project Eyesore Removal was aimed at the town creek, for years a favorite dumping ground. A dozen kids and vigilantes attacked it one Saturday. They removed four dump trucks filled with car parts and two trucks heaped with broken glass, beer bottles, and transgenerational rubbish. The last piece of junk was a rotted tire with a dead rat trapped in the rim. When they lifted the tire, John Leach and Dave Roosa watched a very alive carp float upstream.

The Colonel looked at the carp and thought: A few of these longhairs are allright.

Dave Roosa looked at the carp and thought: At least no one's getting killed or beaten up.

THE Fourth of July was a gala occasion. The American Legion and the Volunteer Fire Department, led by G. M. Allen, paraded flags and firetrucks around the square. The VFW held its annual fireworks display; firecrackers and Roman candles exploded around the courthouse and the police dispatcher was flooded with calls asking if the hippies were shooting up the town again. Harrisonville received its second and third stars from the Missouri Community Betterment Program—for "police protection and leisure time activities."

Jowly Chuck Holder, "recording artist, radio and television personality, KTUL-TV, Tulsa, Oklahoma," presented his Midwest Variety Show at the Lee Theater, just off the square. Merchants held an Old-Fashioned Sale and dressed up in new bib overalls. J.W. Brown wrote an editorial in the *Democrat-Missourian:* "Cass Countians have been able to meet the trend toward a growing suburban community and turn growth into progress." The Lions Club in Peculiar sponsored Bushwhacker Days, with "a cakewalk competition, horses, and minibikes."

The weather stayed hot through July and the Rev. W.T. Niermeier wrote: "The other day I read that I was a WASP. What does WASP stand for? Worried Americans Slowly Perishing? Russia, China, and quite a few misguided residents of this country (I didn't say Americans) seem to hope so . . . The basic problem in all the world, in all areas of life, is that men do not take God and His Word seriously." The Harrisonville School Board announced its dress code for the upcoming school year: hair three inches above the shoulders, no sideburns below the ears, no midriffs or halter tops, hotpants only when covered by a dress, no shirts with any "written or pictorial advertising." The Cass County Junior Livestock Show champion was a 1,060-pound charolais. The West Peculiar Fire Department got a new truck, mounted on a 750 Ford chassis; price: $23,500. Swarms of honeybees drifted over the square and merchants made sure their doors were closed.

Mayor Raine unveiled a new moneymaking plan. The town would sell its water to other communities—2.4 million gallons per month to the Lone Tree Water District for $18,000 a year. Steven Berley, the city manager, sometimes the mayor's punching bag, resigned and told the Kiwanis Club: "We have accomplished a great deal but there is still much to do." The streets needed repairs, he said, and G.M. Allen's Volunteer Fire Department needed a new pumper.

A group of Optimist Club members came back from a convention in Jefferson City and carried out their goal: "to paint the town with optimism." Mayor Raine sat somberly on the front page of the *Democrat-Missourian*, surrounded by dry-cleaned flags and two bovine ladies from the DAR, and proclaimed Constitution Week.

Just before Constitution Week, John Leach got a phone call from a woman who said the Nigger was back on the square. The Colonel sent "one of my men" to check it. The man came back and said Win Allen was sitting up there with a pretty white girl. The Colonel called the police department.

The policeman said: "We know about it. That's why I had my wife call you."

"What do you want me to do, take a hundred and fifty men

up there again?" Leach asked, and hung up.

Finally, after the hottest summer in memory, a storm whirled down from Kansas City; a funnel cloud was seen outside Peculiar. The sirens went off. The townspeople didn't care. There was a lot of thunder and lightning and a few gusts of wind. It rained for three long wonderful hours. The storm saved their crops.

I got back to Harrisonville on Election Day. I drove across country from San Francisco and pushed the tach and the speedometer too much. I wanted to pass through a lot of small towns and get a feel of the land. I leadfooted the car because, for reasons of my own, I wanted to be in Harrisonville when Richard Nixon scored his record landslide. I had a new stockbroker haircut; Harry Jones, a gray-haired friend of mine, one of the *Kansas City Star's* toughest reporters, wrote me a letter and told me to cut my hair if I walked into Harrisonville again. I figured Harry knew what he was talking about.

It was cold and rainy when I got in; an icestorm was on its way. Before long the trees shimmered with crystals of ice . . . Richard Nixon took traditionally Democratic Cass County 9,222 to 3,516 and took Harrisonville 1,657 to 680. The President was the biggest vote-getter. In second place was Sheriff Bill Gough— "our martyred sheriff," prosecutor Don Whitcraft said—getting a few hundred more votes than Congressman William J. Randall. The biggest news, besides the landslide, stretched back to Halloween, when thirty-two tires were slashed at Marvin Burris Ford-Mercury.

Election Day was calm. There was some routine bellyaching . . . a letter in the *Democrat-Missourian* said people couldn't see the Statue of Liberty anymore and the Book of Knowledge was being burned . . . but folks had nothing much to worry about. The land was wet and in good shape, not like Election Day in 1952 when fire chief G.M. Allen issued an emergency warning to the town saying there was an immediate grassfire threat. The hippies weren't hanging around the square anymore, either: Win Allen spent most of his time with a brother in New Mexico; Rise Risner and his father left town for a farm twenty miles away; Gary Hale was having girlfriend problems and he didn't have much time for fist-waving; George Russell moved to Oklahoma.

I spent a lot of time walking the town with my stockbroker hair and black bureaucratic briefcase. Felix Hacker sat in his cubbyholed office and said he didn't like the story in *Rolling Stone* I'd written after my visit in May. He was upset about all "the filthy language" and advised me paternally to go back to California and study the Book of Mormon. He reminisced about his early days in Harrisonville, in the mid 50's: "When I first got here and opened my store, they said—'If you can last two years, you'll make it, but you'll never last two years.' Well, it was rough for two years, but I travailed through and succeeded. Most of the folks in town wouldn't shop with me 'cause I was an outsider. Oh, there are still some things I'm excluded from. I don't get invited to their country club and bridge parties, but I'm not interested in those things anyway." I asked Felix Hacker what he thought the people of Harrisonville had learned by their travail and Felix's eyes twinkled at me. "Well," he said, "we learned we can't trust our own county prosecutor to investigate the conspiracy and we learned it's smart to keep your mouth shut to newsmen."

I went to see Everett Wade, the juvenile officer, and he said the groundskeeper who brought him the hippies' droppings hadn't found much since mid-August, when he brought him a pack of "revolutionary form-fitting prophylactics." Everett Wade held up the pack of prophylactics and smirked. "Revolutionary rubbers!" he said. " 'Course," he added, "not much has changed and it won't change either while we've got these" and handed me a neatly typed list of the Warren Court's decisions.

I went to see Police Chief Bill Davis and when I gave the dispatcher my name, a group of policemen followed me into his office. I sat across from him and Bill Davis grinned at me. I asked him about the conspiracy and he grinned. I asked him about the hippies and he grinned. I asked him about the town's progress and he grinned. I asked him if he'd answer any of my questions and he said: "Nope!" The word bounced at me from many people for several weeks.

I spent some time sitting around the Chamber of Commerce office, chit-chatting with the secretary, who is the town gossip. The Chamber of Commerce is across the hall from the real-estate millionaire who told the vigilantes he'd pay all their court costs whatever the charges. The secretary didn't know I'd written the *Rolling Stone* story and fed me titillating pieces of town history. Did I know Cole Younger, their Robin Hood badman, never got married? Did I know Cole's father was a slaveowner? Did I know Cole Younger's only direct descendants were some Nigrow people who came down from Kansas City once for a Younger family reunion?

I drove up to Kansas City to see Jan Roosa and Gene Wagner. We sat around and drank a lot of Jan's bourbon and scotch, and near the end of the long evening Gene Wagner stretched out on the floor and rubbed his cavernous eyes. "Four people get killed in the street," he said, "and nobody gives a shit. The town doesn't give a shit, the kids don't give a shit, the federal government doesn't give a shit. Step over the bodies, baby, go about your business." Jan Roosa looked kindly at his friend and said: "I told you it would be like that all along. You, the virginal idealist, you wouldn't believe me."

The next day I went to visit Charlie Simpson. The trees were

nearly straightjacketed with frost; the wind hissed and whipped
to the bone; a gas station attendant told me it was "cold enough
to freeze the balls off a brass monkey." I drove around Holden,
went to Herb's Drive-In, found the junkyard, drove over to Chilhowee, and passed the sign that says: "Nixon Feeds." I love that
sign. I found the cemetery after going into the truckstop down
the road and meeting the waitress with the black eye. She pointed
toward the graveyard and I walked down there looking for his
grave. I don't exactly know why I went there. I was freezing cold,
the graveyard is as flat as a football field, and I couldn't find
Charlie's stone. I walked up and down a few times and finally said
"Fuck it!" and left.

I drove back to Harrisonville to see the Colonel. I was ner-
vous about John Leach; Harry Jones had told me: "Be careful,
some of those boys are pretty rough." I found the Colonel in his
gas station. He clapped me on the back, held my hand, and said
I was his hero. I'd never been called a hero by a vigilante before;
I thought it was some kind of country sarcasm and asked him
what he meant.

The Colonel said he'd loved the *Rolling Stone* story. He
loved it so much he'd xeroxed 1,500 copies and spread it all over
town. It showed what dirty words the hippies used and how they
drank and smoked marijuana. It showed what moneychangers and
pigeon-dealers the merchants were. The Colonel handed me the
greatest compliment he could think of. "You know," he said, "if
it weren't for your story, I don't think we could have stirred folks
up to take over the square."

We went to his home and his wife kissed me; the Colonel
showed me his old books and a picture of his father in Army
uniform riding a snow-white horse; he called me "old buddy."
The next day I went back to his gas station and he gave me a stack
of letters he kept in a strongbox with his money and his gun. I

read them sitting next to his cash-register, being gladhanded and thumped on the back by vigilantes who came in for boxes of shells . . . the deer season was starting.

> *Dear Colonel Leach,*
> *Thank God for the men in Harrisonville. I had been wonder-ing if there were any real men left. Now if we could get a bunch of you in Washington, D.C. maybe we could get our wonderful men back in order. How about having a hippie roundup all over? And send all the hippies over to Red China. Good idea, don't you think?*
>
> > *Thanks again for making my day brighter.*
> > *May God bless you all.*

> *Dear Sir:*
> *I want to express my congratulations to you for a job well done. If every city in America would do what you've done in Harrisonville, we wouldn't have all the turmoil that is created by the hippie movement. I know that is a hard way to do it but I am afraid that is the only way to get the job done. And let me be one of the first to congratulate you.*

> *Dear Colonel Leach and Chief Davis,*
> *I'm writing this from Emporia, Kansas. In our town, all we have are signs in eating places that say—No shirts, no socks, no eats. I would have liked to have been there with some sheep shears and started in on that Win Allen and the bunch that carried the coffin of the SOB that killed the policemen. Keep up the good work. Have thought about getting a bunch together here just to use a pair of shears. Most of these people cannot accept discipline. It's about time they were told to do something and forced to do it.*

I finished the letters and stared out John Leach's gas station window at the icicles on the trees.

"Yes sir, Joe," the Colonel said, "you really helped us with our situation here."

"Well," I asked him, "you think the town's learned anything by all this?"

A man came through the door and he said: "Hey, Colonel. I can't get the damn dates staight. Are we shooting buck today or does that start tomorrow?"

"Any deer," the Colonel told him, "that's what the book says."

I repeated my question.

"Naw," John Leach said, "not a lot. The merchants still care only about their money and the prosecutor still doesn't have the guts to open up the conspiracy. But then we scared the hippies away and I think that's gonna happen all over the country. They're not gonna try to build any Woodstock Nation no more. I saw in the paper that *Abeee* Hoffman's hanging it up, too. This is one war we just about won."

A man came in waving a rifle and talking about shooting a buck at 300 yards with a Winchester 70 in a .375 H and H Magnum. "That old buck just flopped down," the man said, and I said goodbye.

I got into my car and made the tach jump. Ice hung off the trees and sleet was falling hard. I couldn't see too well and around me the woods echoed with hunters' gunfire.

About the Author

JOE ESZTERHAS was born in Csakanydoroszlo, Hungary, on November 23, 1944. He grew up in refugee camps and in the American Midwest. He attended Ohio University and was an award-winning reporter/columnist for the *Cleveland Plain Dealer* from 1967 to 1971. He was fired for criticizing his employer in an article which appeared in the *Evergreen Review*. He fled the Midwest with his wife and dog and now lives in San Francisco, where he is an editor of *Rolling Stone*.